THE STORY OF A RED DEER

THE STORY
OF A RED DEER

J. W. Fortescue

CANONGATE • KELPIES

First published 1897 by MacMillan and Co. Ltd.
First published in Kelpies 1988
Published In Canada by Optimum Publishing
International (1984) Inc., Montreal

Cover illustration by Alexa Rutherford

Printed in Great Britain
by Cox & Wyman Ltd, Reading, Berkshire

ISBN 0 86241 174 2

*The publishers acknowledge the financial assistance
of the Scottish Arts Council in the
publication of this volume*

CANONGATE PUBLISHING LTD
17 JEFFREY STREET, EDINBURGH EH1 1DR

THE EPISTLE DEDICATORY.

To

MR. HUGH FORTESCUE,

HONOURED SIR,

When in the spring of this present year you asked of me that I should write you a book, I was at the first not a little troubled; for of making of many books there is no end, and of making of good books but small beginning; and albeit there be many heroes of our noble county of Devon, whose lives, if worthily written, might exceed in value all other books (saving always those that are beyond price) that might be placed in the hands of the youth thereof for instruction and example, yet for such a task I deemed myself all too poorly fitted; for if men would write books to be read of the young, they must write them, not after particular study, but from the fulness and the overflowing of their knowledge of such things as they have dwelt withal and felt and loved beyond all others.

So at the last I bethought me that there was no book that I could more profitably write for you than the life of one of our own red deer, which, as they be of the most beautiful of all creatures to the eye, so be also the most worthy of study by the mind for their subtlety, their nobility and their wisdom. For though I would have you love the stories of great men and take delight in the reading of good books, yet I would have you take no less delight in the birds and the beasts that share with you your home, and in the observance of their goings out and their comings in, of their friends and of their enemies, of their prosperities and of their perils ; whereby you will gain not only that which the great Mr. Milton (in his tract of Education) hath called the helpful experiences of hunters, fowlers and fishermen, but such a love of God's creatures as will make the world the fuller of joys for you because the fuller of friends ; and this not in one wise only, for I have ever noticed that they which be fondest of dumb creatures are given to be tenderest to their fellow-men.

So here you have the life of a wild red deer, set

down with such poor skill as I possess, even as the deer have told it to me in many a long ride and many a stirring chase, and as they have told it to all others that would listen, to such great hunters of old as the noble Count Gaston de Foix and the worthy Sieur Jacques du Fouilloux, and to many friends, of whom some indeed are passed away, but many yet remain, striving ever to hear more of the same story.   And if my tale be short, yet blame me not, for it is for yourself by your own learning of the deer to enlarge and to enrich it ; so that when your nine years are waxed to threescore and nine, you may take down this small volume and write it anew, out of the treasures of a fuller knowledge than mine own, for the generations that shall come after you in this our ancient and well-beloved home.

And so not doubting of your kindly acceptance hereof, I bid you heartily farewell, being always

Your very loving kinsman and faithful friend to serve you

J. W. F.

Castle Hill.
This 26th of September, 1897.

THE STORY OF A RED-DEER

CHAPTER I

ONCE upon a time there was a little Red-Deer Calf. You know what a Red-Deer is, for you of all boys have been brought up to know, though it may be that you have never seen a calf very close to you. A very pretty little fellow he was, downy-haired and white-spotted, though as yet his legs were rather long and his ears were rather large, for he was still only a very few weeks old. But he did not think himself a baby by any means, for he was an early calf and had been born in the second week in May; and a birthday in the second week in May is the greatest event that can occur in a Red-Deer's family.

The first thing that he remembered was that he found himself lying very snug and warm in a patch of fern, with the most beautiful pair of brown eyes that ever were seen gazing straight down upon him.

And soon he was aware that they were the eyes of
the Hind his mother, that they followed him where-
ever he went, and watched over him whatever he did,
and that, whatever he might want, she was there to
provide it for him. She always had a cosy bed ready
for him in grass or fern ; she washed him clean and
brushed his little coat with her tongue every
morning ; and she taught him but two lessons—to lie
as still as a mouse, and to do just as he was bid.
For every morning before dawn she had to go afield
to feed herself, farther than the little Calf could
travel with her ; and as she had no nurse to leave
in charge of him, she just tucked him up as closely
as she could, and told him to lie still till she came
back. And like a good little fellow he obeyed her ;
which was well for him, for if he had taken it into
his head to jump up and look about him, some evil
man or beast might have seen him and made away
with him ; and then this story would never have
been written.

Always just before the sun rose she came
back, and every day she seemed to love him better,
and every day he felt that she was more than
the whole world to him. And morning after morning up rose the blessed sun, and drove the mist away,

and sent a little ray forward through the fern to kiss him and bid him good-morrow. And the mist left a drop on every blade and blossom, and said, "Good-bye, my little fellow; I shall come back again this evening;" and the drops nodded and sparkled and twinkled, and kept whispering, "Yes, coming back this evening," over and over again, till the sun said that he could stand it no longer and was obliged to dry them all up. Then rose a hum of many wings as the flies woke up, and went out for their day's work; but the breeze moved like a sentry over the bed of the little Calf and said to them, "Move on, move on; this little Calf must not be disturbed;" and they dared not disobey, for they knew that, if they did, he was certain sooner or later to send for his big brother, the Westerly Gale, who would blow them away with a vengeance. And all through the day the breeze kept singing through the graceful, yielding grass and the stubborn wiry heather; while mingled with it came snatches of a little song from the brown peat-stream in the combe below him. He could not make out much of it except these words, which came over and over again:

> Mother and child come here, come here,
> I am the friend of the Wild Red-Deer.

For some time they moved but little distant from the place where he was born, for his legs could not yet carry him very far ; but as he grew stronger they wandered farther, till at last one day he found himself on high ground, and saw the world that he was to live in, his heritage of Exmoor. You know it, for you have seen it, fold upon fold of grass and heather, slashed by deep combes and merry babbling streams, and bounded on the one hand by the blue sky and on the other by the blue sea. It was all his own, for he was a wild Red-Deer. And he looked upon it with his great round eyes, and pricked his ears and tossed his little head ; for the sun was shining warm above him, and the soft west wind blew fresh and untainted over the sea and flew across the moor, catching up all that was sweetest on its way from grass and gorse and heather, and bearing it straight to his nostrils. And he threw his little nose into the air and snuffed up the full, rich breeze ; for no creature has a finer scent than a deer ; and he felt that this was life indeed.

Then they went down, leaving the song of the wind ever fainter behind them ; and in its stead rose the song of the peat-stream bidding them come down to it. So they went ; and there it was trickling down as clear as crystal, though as yellow as amber. There was but little water in it that fine midsummer, but it hastened on none the less over the stones in a desperate hurry, as are all Exmoor streams, to get to the sea. And it whispered its song as it went, but so low that they heard no words. They passed by a little shallow, and there the Calf saw dozens of little fry, scurrying about from stone to stone; and just below the shallow they came to a little brown, oily pool in a basin of rock. The Calf looked into it, and there he saw his own little form, and behind it his mother's sweet eyes watching over him. And then for the first time he noticed that his own coat was spotted while his mother's was red. But while he was staring at the water a fly suddenly came, and began to dance a reel over it to show what a fine fellow he was, when all of a sudden a neat little body, all brown and gold and red spots, leaped up out of the water, seized the fly in his mouth and fell back with a splash which broke the pretty picture all to pieces.

He shrank back, for he was rather startled, but his mother soon comforted him. "It was only a little Trout, my dear," she said, "only a greedy little Trout."

"But he was such a pretty little fellow," he said, for he had quite got over his fright; "I wish he would jump again."

But the Hind looked grave. "We are never unkind to the Trout," she said, "for they belong to the peat-stream, but you must never become familiar with them. Fallow-Deer, I believe, treat them as equals," and here she looked very proud, "but we do not. They are a lazy lot of fellows whose fore-fathers would not take the trouble to go down to the sea, whereby they might have grown into noble fish, with a coat as bright as the moon on the water. But they would not, and so they have remained small and ugly, and they never lose their spots. You must never be rude to them, for that would be un-worthy of a Red-Deer, but you must never make great friends with them. You may talk to little Salmon when we see them, for they lose their spots, but not to the Trout." For the Hind was a great lady, with much pride of race, which though it made her civil to every one, taught her to be shy of idlers and low company.

"But, mother," said the poor little Calf, "*I've* got a spotted coat."

"But you will lose it, my darling," she said

tenderly. "No, no, my child will be a true Red-Deer."

So they left the water, and presently stopped while his mother plucked at a tuft of sweet grass among the heather ; when to his astonishment a little grey ball of fur came bounding out of a hole in the ground, and another at his heels, and three more after them. And they ran round and round and played like mad things. And presently another, far bigger than they, came up slowly out of another hole, sat up on her hind-legs, pricked her ears, and began to look about her. Then catching sight of the Calf she crouched down, and began in a very shrill voice : "Why, my dear tender heart" (for she was not only a Rabbit, but a Devonshire Rabbit, and of course spoke broad Devon), "if it isn't my little maister, and her ladyship too, begging your pardon, my lady. And sweetly pretty he is, my lady ; and butiful you'm looking too, in your summer coat, so glossy as a chestnut, sure enough. And dear heart alive, how he groweth. Why, 'twas but a few days agone that my Bucky saith to me—I don't rightly remember how many days agone, but I mind 'twas the very day when the old Greyhen up to Badg-worthy came to ask me if I had seen her poult—for she's lost a poult, my lady, hath the poor soul, as your ladyship knoweth. Well, my Bucky saith to me, 'Bunny,' saith he, 'you may depend that young maister will grow to be so fine a stag as ever was seen on Exmoor.'" Then without pausing an instant she called out at the top of her voice to one of the little rabbits: "Flossy-a! Come back, little bittlehead, come back, or the fox will catch 'ee!"

The Hind listened very graciously to this long speech, for she loved to hear good words of her Calf, and she was just a *little* pleased to hear of her own good looks. But she could not help looking beautiful, and she looked all the more so because she very seldom thought about it. So she returned the compliment by asking after Bunny and her family.

"Oh! thank you, my lady," answered Bunny, "I reckon we'm well. There han't been no man this way this long time, thanks be; and there's plenty of meat, and not too much rain. And the family's well, my lady; look to mun playing all around, so gay ; and my third family this spring, my lady—that I should say so! No, I reckon I can't complain ; but oh, my lady! they foxes, and they weasels! They do tell me that the old vixen from Cornham Brake

hath five cubs ; and I can't abide a vixen—never
could. And they weasels—they'm small, but they'm
worse than foxes. Now there's my Bucky. He
can't bide home, he saith, these fine days, but must
go and lie out. I says to mun, 'Bucky,' I says, ''tis
very well for the likes of her ladyship to lie out every
day, but *you* should bide home to bury.' But no, he
would go. 'Well then, Bucky,' I says, 'I reckon
that you'll grow a pair of horns like his lordship, brow,
bay, and trey, Bucky,' I says, 'and turn to bay when
the weasel's after 'ee.' And with that he layeth back
his ears and away he goeth—Flossy-a, come back,
will 'ee, or I'll give you what vor ! Now there's that
Flossy, my lady, so like to her father as my two ears.
She won't bide close to bury; and they do tell me
that the vixen to Cornham has moved this way. It
won't do, my lady, it won't do. Oh dear, dear,
dear !" And she stopped for want of breath.

"Well, good evening, Bunny," said the Hind
very kindly, "I must take my little son home. I
shall see you again very soon."

"And good evening to your ladyship," answered
Bunny, "and good evening to you, my pretty dear.
Ah ! you'm his lordship's son sure enough. I mind
the time——"

But the Hind had moved on out of hearing, for when once an old Doe-Rabbit begins to talk she never stops. Then presently the Calf said: " Mother, who is his lordship?" And she answered: "He is your father, my darling. For the Red-Deer are lords of this forest, and he is the lord of them all. And brow, bay, trey is the coronet that every good Stag wears, and which you too shall wear in due time, when you grow up." And he said no more, for to his mind there was nothing on earth half so beautiful as she was, and he asked no better than to grow up to be such another.

CHAPTER II

Now the very next day the Hind led her Calf away from the combe where they lay; and after travelling some little way, they met the most beautiful bird that the Calf had ever seen. His plumage was all of glossy black, which shone blue and green and purple in the sun, while to set it off he had a patch of pure white on each wing, and a spot of red above each eye; his tail was forked and bent outwards in two graceful curves, and his legs were feathered to the very heel. He flew towards them some little way, with an easy noiseless flight, and lighted just in front of them, as handsome a fellow as you will see in a summer's day.

"Well, good Master Blackcock," said the Hind, "has my lord not moved?"

"Not a step, my lady," said the bird; "he lieth so quiet as my wife when she's sitting, though the flies do worrit mun terrible."

"Then come along, son," she said. And she led him on and presently stopped and whispered, "Look." And there he saw such a sight as he had never dreamed of; a great Stag nearly twice the size of his mother, with horns half grown and the velvet black with flies, lying down motionless but for constant twitching of his head. The Calf could not see how big he was, till presently he rose on to his feet, and stretched himself, throwing his horns right back, with a mighty yawn. Then he stood for a minute or two blinking rather sleepily, but always shaking his head and wincing under the torment of the flies. His back was as broad as a bullock's and his coat shone with good living; and the little Calf, looked with all his eyes, for he had made up his mind then and there to stand just like that and to stretch himself just like that, when he had grown to be such a fine stag as that.

But presently the Hind led him away and asked the Blackcock, "And where is my sister?" And the Blackcock led them on, and after a time, to the Calf's delight, they came in sight of two more Hinds and another little Calf. And all three caught the wind of them and came forward to meet them. One of the Hinds was very big and grey, and she had no

Calf, but the other was smaller and bright red, and
had at her foot as sweet a little Calf as ever you saw;
and it was the smaller of the two Hinds that came to
them first. Then both of the mothers laid their
Calves down, and began to talk, but they had hardly
exchanged a word, when the old grey Hind broke in.

"So it's you, Tawny, is it?" she said; "and you
have brought a Calf with you, I see. I suppose I
must ask, is it a stag or a hind?"

"A stag, Aunt Yeld," said the Lady Tawny (for
that was the name of our Calf's mother); "do look
at him for a minute. He does look so sweet in his
bed."

"A stag, is it?" said Aunt Yeld with a little sniff.
"Well, I suppose if people must have calves they had
better have stags. Ruddy's here is a hind, but I
never could see the attraction of any calf myself."
For Aunt Yeld, like some old maids (but by no
means like all) that have no children of their own,
thought it the right thing to look down on Calves;
and indeed she was rather a formidable old lady.
She had two very big tushes in her upper jaw, which
she was constantly showing, and she made a great
point (when she was not flurried) of closing the claws
of her hoofs very tight, and letting her hind-feet fall

exactly where her fore-feet had fallen, which she knew to be the way of a stag.

"And now that you have brought your calves here," continued Aunt Yeld, "I may as well tell you that the sooner you take them away the better, for there is a Greyhen here with a brood, who never ceases to pester me with enquiries about a poult which she has lost. It's not my business to look after people's poults; if they can't take care of them themselves, they had better not have them, I say. The bird's an idiot, I think. I questioned her pretty closely, and she really seemed not very clear whether she had really lost a poult or not."

But the two Mother-Hinds looked at their calves and said :

"Poor thing;" and Ruddy's Calf, which was feeling perhaps a little lonely, uttered a plaintive little bleat.

"Ruddy," said Aunt Yeld severely, "if your child is going to make that noise, I really must request you to—bless my heart, there's that Greyhen again. No, bird, I have *not* seen your poult."

And there sure enough was the poor old Greyhen, looking sadly dowdy when compared with her mate, the Blackcock, with half a dozen fluffy little poults round her. She was evidently anxious, for she turned her head so quickly this way and that to keep them all in sight that it nearly made the Calves giddy.

"Oh, I beg your pardon, my lady," she said very humbly, and turned round. But the Lady Tawny walked after her, and asked what was the matter.

"Oh, my lady," said the Greyhen, "I didn't mean no harm, but do 'ee tell me, have 'ee seen my little poult? My lady Yeld axed me so many questions that I got fairly mazed, and I've counted my poults times and times till I hardly know how many they be. For I'm not so young as I was, my lady, and I've brought up many families. My first mate he was shot, if you mind, my lady; butiful bird he was too. And a pigeon passed just now and I axed him to count, but they never have but two eggs in their nestes, he saith, so he can't count more than two. And the old Bucky was nigh here, and I axed he. 'Bless your life, neighbour,' he saith, 'my Bunny has so many children that I've a given up counting.' But it's not for me to stand talking with your ladyship; though there's one poult missing, I'm sure of that."

"Poor soul," said the Hind very gently, "I am

afraid that I have not seen your poult. I am so sorry."

" Ah! bless your ladyship's kind heart," said the Greyhen. " You was always—mercy on us, there 'a is. Stand over them, my lady, for mercy's sake, stand over them." And she crouched close to the ground with abject terror in her eyes, while the poults, frightened to death, hid themselves all round her.

For far above them against the glorious blue sky hung a little speck, with quick, nervous wings that fluttered and paused, and fluttered and paused. And it slanted down to right, and slanted back to left, as though it had been swung by a cord from the heavens; then it fluttered its wings and paused once more. But the Hind stood over the Greyhen and poults, so that they should not be seen; and all the time the Greyhen kept gasping out little broken words.

" Oh, they blue Hawks! Oh, they blue Hawks! Oh, the roog! 'Twas he that did it—sure enough —Oh, the blue roog!"

Then the little speck made a great lunge forward, fluttered for a moment, and passed away out of sight; and the Hind stepped back very gently, and said:

"Quite safe now. Good-day, mistress. Take care of the poults."

"Bless your kind heart, and good-day to your ladyship," answered the Greyhen. "I have six poults yet, I'm sure 'tis six now, and that's a many to wash and tend and feed; but when they'm grown you may depend they shall always help your ladyship, if I can teach them. Good-day, my lady, and thank you, and may you have good luck with your blessed little son."

Now all this time you may be sure that the Hind had kept a constant eye towards the spot where her Calf was lying, the more so since she could see Aunt Yeld peering through the grass at him. So she went straight back to kiss him as soon as the Greyhen was gone, lest Aunt Yeld's grey face might have frightened him; but he wasn't frightened at her in the least. And Aunt Yeld for two whole steps quite forgot to walk like a stag, and said, "I must do you the justice to observe, Tawny, that he is a very handsome little fellow." Then she turned away, blowing out her lips to show her tushes and putting on the stag's gait as nearly as she could, and made a vicious bite at a little blade of grass, as she had seen Stags bite at a turnip; which did not become her pretty neck (for

Hinds are always pretty, however old) half as much as the graceful nibble which was natural to her. But it was all make-believe, and if she had spoken her heart she would have said : " I think that your Calf is the greatest darling I ever saw, and oh, how I wish I were you ! "

Then Aunt Yeld turned round and said : " Now you two mustn't think of going. You are not fit to take care of yourselves, so you must stay with me, and I'll take care of you." You see she had quite forgotten what she said at first, for she had really a kind heart, though nothing could keep her from patronising every one.

So for many days they lived together, and Aunt Yeld always posted herself up wind of them to keep watch over them ; and if our soldiers in their red coats were sentries half as good as she, they would be the best in the world. Now and again, though very seldom, the great Stag would join them and lie by them all day, chewing the cud and shaking his great head, which grew bigger every day. But he never uttered a word, unless it was to say, " Very good that growing wheat was this morning, to be sure," to which the Hind would answer, " I am so glad, dearest ; " or it would be, " The turnips on Yarner farm are not coming on well in this dry weather, I am told; it's very annoying, for I was looking forward to my turnips," and then the Hind would say, " I am so sorry, dearest. How I hope it will rain soon!" For old stags are perhaps rather too fond of their dinners.

Once only he showed himself quite different, and that was when one day the Blackcock flew up to say that all the hills were coming down. Now the way the Blackcock got the idea into his head was this. He had been taking a bath in the dust at the foot of a great sheet of screes, the loose, flat stones on the hill-side which you have often seen on the moor, and had enjoyed it greatly, fluffing out his feathers and flapping his great wings. But while he was in the middle of it a Jackdaw came flying overhead, and seeing this great ball of feathers rolling about, pitched down upon the screes to see what strange thing it might be. And as he came hopping down to look at it closer, he displaced one little stone, which displaced another little stone, and that another, until quite a number of stones were set moving, and came rushing down for twenty feet like a tiny cataract, close to the Blackcock's ear. Whereupon the Jackdaw flapped off cawing with fright, and the Blackcock flew away screaming to tell the deer that all the hills were coming down.

But when he came the old Stag stood up at once and said : "Lady Yeld, take the lead ; Ruddy and Tawny, follow her. Steadily now, no hurrying !" Then they moved on a little way and stopped, the Stag always remaining behind them ; for they could see that the hills were not coming down before them, and therefore they must have begun to fall behind them, if the Blackcock spoke truth. And that was why the Stag remained behind, to be nearest to the danger, as a gentleman should be. And some day, if you go into the army, you will learn that in a retreat the rearguard is the post of greatest danger ; and you must read the story of the retreat of Sir John Moore's army to Corunna and Vigo, and see what great things Uncle Charlie's regiment did there.

The Deer stopped for a time, and at last the Stag said: "I can see nothing, hear nothing, and wind nothing. Are you *quite* sure the hills are all coming down, Blackcock ? I think that you must have made some mistake." For the old Stag was a great gentleman, and always very civil and courteous. But Aunt Yeld, who was quick of temper, stamped on the ground, and said almost out loud : " Bah ! I believe the bird's as great an idiot as his wife."

The Blackcock looked very foolish, and was so much confused that he did not know what to answer ; but the Lady Tawny said kindly : " Thank you, Black-cock, for coming. You mustn't let us keep you from your dinner." And though it was not his dinner-time, he was so glad of the excuse that he flew straight away to his wife, and told her all about it. But all she said was : " So you went and told his lord-ship, did 'ee ; and what about me and my poults if the world cometh to an end ? It's like 'ee, it is, to go disturbing her blessed ladyship and her sweet little son with your stories. But never a word for me, oh dear me no, who slave for the poults morning, noon, and night ; oh dear, oh dear," and so on for half an hour, till the Blackcock almost made up his mind never to have a dust-bath again. For the poults had been rather troublesome that morning, and the Grey-hen's temper was a little upset in consequence. Thus you see that the Blackcock had an unpleasant time of it ; and perhaps it served him right.

But except on this one occasion the Stag never bestirred himself ; behaving very lazily, as I have told you, and never opening his mouth except to munch

his food or talk of it. He never spoke a word to the
Calf, for old stags are not very fond of calves ; and
you may be sure that the Calf never said a word to
him, for he was terribly afraid of him ; nor was he
far wrong, for an old stag, while his head is growing,
is almost as irritable as an old gentleman with a gouty
toe. The only difference between the two is this,
that the stag can eat and drink as much as he pleases,
and do nothing but good to his head, while the more
a gouty old gentleman eats and drinks, the worse for
his toe. And it is just because they cannot eat and
drink as much as they please that gouty old gentle-
men are more irritable than stags ; and I for one
don't pity them, for a man is made to think of better
things than his food and drink.

But if he could not talk to the Stag, he made
great friends with Ruddy's Calf, who was the
sweetest, gentlest little thing that you can imagine.
And though she was a little smaller than he was, she
could do nearly everything that he could. They
ran races, and they tried which could jump the
higher and which could spring the farther, and she
was as fast and as active as he was. But one day he
must needs make her try which could butt the other
the harder. So they butted each other gently two

or three times, and he liked it so much that he took a great run and butted her hard, and hurt her, though he had not meant it. Then she cried, "Maa-a-a! You're very rude and rough. It's a shame to treat a little hind so; I sha'n't play any more." Of course they soon made it up again, but his mother told him to remember that she was only a little hind. And he remembered it, but he could not help thinking that it was far better to be a little stag.

CHAPTER III

ONE day they were lying out in the grass as usual, and our little Calf was having a great game of romps with the little Hind. The Stag was not with them, but Aunt Yeld was standing sentry, when all of a sudden she came back in a great fluster, not at all like a stag, as she was always trying to be.

" Quick, quick, quick ! " she said. " I can wind them and I can see them. Call your Calves and let us go. Quick, quick ! "

Then the two mothers rose up in a terrible fright. " Quick," said Aunt Yeld again. " Run away as fast as you can ! "

" But our Calves can't keep up if we go fast," pleaded the two mothers.

" Bless the Calves, I never thought of that," said Aunt Yeld. " Wait a minute ; look ! "

Then they looked down across the rolling waves of grass flecked by the shadows of the flying clouds, and a mile and a half away they saw a moving white mass, with a dark figure before it and another dark figure behind it. The mass stood in deep shadow, for a cloud hung over it ; but the cloud passed away and then the sun flashed down upon it, and what the Deer saw (for they have far better eyes than you or I) was this. Twenty-five couples of great solemn hounds trotting soberly over the heather with a horseman in a white coat at their heads and another at their sterns, and the coats of hounds and horses shining as glossy as their own. A fresh puff of wind bore a wave of strange scent to the nostrils of the Deer, and our little Calf snuffed it and thought it the most unpleasant that he had ever tasted. " Remember it, my son," whispered his mother to him, " nasty though it be, and beware of it."

But Aunt Yeld stood always a little in advance, talking to herself. " I passed just in front of the place where they are now on my way back from breakfast this morning," she murmured. " I trust that scent has failed by this time. Ah ! "

And as she spoke some of the hounds swung suddenly with one impulse towards them, but the horseman behind them galloped forward quick as thought, and turned them back ; and there came on the wind the sound of a shrill yelp, which made all three of the Hinds to quiver again. Then the mass began to move faster than before, and the Deer watched it go further and further away from them till at last it settled down to its first pace and vanished out of sight.

"Well, that is a mercy," said Aunt Yeld with a deep sigh. "I thought it was full early yet for those detestable creatures to begin their horrible work again. I think that we are safe now, but I'll just make sure in case of accidents."

And with that she began to trot about in the strangest fashion. For she made a great circle to the track by which she had come back from feeding in the early morning, and ran back along it for some way, and then she turned off it, and after a time made another circle which brought her to a little stream. Then she ran up the water and made another circle which brought her back again.

"There," she said, "if they do follow us, that will puzzle them." But the Lady Tawny had been looking at her Calf all the time, and now she spoke : "I am afraid to stay here any longer, Aunt Yeld. I will take my Calf far away to a quiet spot that I know of, and do you stop with sister and look after her."

So they parted, and very sad they were at parting. She led her Calf away slowly, that he might not tire, but they had not gone very far when there ran past them a great Buck-Rabbit. He neither saw nor heard them, for his eyes were starting out of his head with fright; and he went on only for a little way and then lay down and squealed most miserably. Then they heard a faint sound rather like the yelp that they had heard from the hound, but much smaller; and presently there came five little bits of brown bodies, long, and lithe and slender, racing along on their tiny short legs far faster than you would have thought possible. They were following the line of the Rabbit, and the old mother Weasel led the way, speaking to the scent as loud as she could (and that was not very loud), "Forward, children, forward, forward," and the four little Weasels joined in chorus, "Forward, forward, forward"; then she cried, "Blood, children, blood," and they answered at the top of their pipes, "Blood, blood, blood, blood." And their fierce little eyes flashed, and their sharp little teeth gleamed as they dashed away through the grass; and I am afraid that the Buck-Rabbit had but a poor chance with them, though he was nearly as big as the whole five of them put together. For I suppose that, for its size, there is no creature on earth so fierce and blood-thirsty as a weasel; but remember, too, that he is also the pluckiest little beast that there is, and would fight you and me if we drove him too far.

The Calf was very much puzzled. "Why doesn't the Rabbit run on, mother, if he is afraid of the Weasels?" he said. "I should have run on as far as I could. Will they leave him alone because he lies down and squeals?"

But she answered sadly, "No, no! and, my son, if ever it should befall you that you must run for your life, as I fear may be only too likely, then keep up a brave heart and run on till you can run no more."

And he answered, "Yes, mother," and thought to himself that he would fight to the end too; for he hoped one day to grow into a good stag and have horns to fight with; and besides he was a brave little fellow. And, for my part, I think that the Calf was right; and if (as I hope may never be) after you are grown up, disappointment should lie in wait for you at every turn, and fate and your own fault should hunt you to despair, then run on bravely, and when you can run no more, face them and dare them to do their worst; but never, never, never lie down and squeal.

So they journeyed on for three whole days, often stopping that the Calf might rest. And on the third day as they were passing along one side of a combe, they saw another strange sight. For on the other side the rock came through the soil, and there at the foot of the rock stood a ruddy-coloured creature with a white throat, and prick ears, and a sharp nose, and a bushy tail that tapered to a point and ended in a white tag. She carried a rabbit in her mouth, and round her stood five little Cubs, jumping and scrambling and playing, and crying out, " Rabbit for dinner, rabbit for dinner!" For a time she looked at them with the rabbit still in her mouth while they danced around her, till presently one ran up behind one of his brothers and rolled him over, and the other lay on his back kicking and struggling while the first pretended to kill him; and then a third came up and caught one of them by the scruff of the neck and made him open his mouth so wide that you would have thought he could never have shut it again. And then the old Vixen laid the rabbit on the ground, and said, " Worry, worry, worry!" and the Cubs dashed at it and began biting at it and tearing, and pulling, and scratching, till they rent it all to pieces. Then one little fellow got hold of a whole hind-leg and ran away to eat it by himself, and the rest cried out, "Greedy, greedy!" and ran after him to take it from him; and they scuffled and worried and snarled till you would have thought that they meant to eat each other up as well as the rabbit. But it was only play, though rough play, for Foxes are rough fellows; and all the time the old Vixen sat on her haunches smiling and saying, "That's my little Cubs! that's my little Cubs!"

Then the Hind and Calf passed on, and she led him into a great deep wood of oak-coppice, where there was hardly a tree that was not oak, except now and again a mountain-ash. And they passed through the bright silver stems of the young trees and under the heavy foliage of the old ones; till they saw a mountain-ash shake its golden berries over their heads, and came to a hollow where a tiny stream came trickling down, almost hidden among hart's-tongues. There she laid him down; and this wood was their new home.

Soon after, the dry weather came to an end, and the South-West wind came laden with rain from the sea. But the Hind and Calf lay sheltered in the wood, and heard the wind singing above them, and saw the scud drifting slowly in great columns down the valley. They roamed far through the wood, for it seemed to cover the valley's side for miles, and he watched her as she looked about for ivy, which was her favourite food, and envied her when she reared up to pluck some tempting morsel hanging from the oak trees. Nor would he let her have all the good things to herself, for he would nuzzle at the green leaves between her lips and pretend to enjoy them greatly.

A very happy peaceful life it was, for they were never disturbed, though occasionally they saw company. They had not been there but very few days, when very early in the morning they saw the old Vixen come stealing into the wood with a Cub in her mouth. She looked so weary and footsore, that though deer do not like rough, unmannerly creatures such as foxes, which feed on flesh, the Hind could not help saying, "Why, Mrs. Vicky, you look dreadfully tired."

But the Vixen hardly turned her head, and then only to answer very roughly, "No, I am not tired, I am not tired," though after a time she added "thank you" in rather a surly tone; for in Devon nobody is altogether uncivil. And she went plodding on.

"Have they been disturbing your earth?" asked the Hind. "I hope the Cubs are all well." Then the Vixen could not help stopping to say: "Yes, they'm well. This is the last of mun. Twenty mile and more have I gone back and 'vor with mun this blessed night. They was rather a late litter, you see, and I was obliged to carry mun. But I'm not tired, oh no, I am not tired—my lady." And she went on again doggedly with her Cub, though they could see that she was so tired that she could hardly move. And let me tell you that it was a great stretch of civility for the Vixen to call the Hind "my lady," for Foxes are very independent, and like a great many other people think that they must show their independence by being uncivil; whereby they only prevent others from seeing what brave, patient creatures they really are.

The very next morning they saw a new visitor come in, a grey old person as big as the Vixen, with a long sharp nose, and a deal of white about his face, a very little short tail, and four short clumsy legs. He was waddling along slowly, and grumbling to himself: "'Tisn't often that I spake, but spake I will. 'Tis mortal hard that he should come and take my house. 'Tis my house, I made mun, and I digged mun. 'Tisn't right; 'tisn't rasonable."

" What is it, old Grey ? " said the Hind.

The Badger looked up and stared. Then he said very slowly " Aw ! " drawing out the word till he could collect his wits. " Well, look 'ee, 'tis like this. Two days agone,—I think 'twas two days—the old Dog-Fox—you know mun, he that hath so much white to his brush—well, he cometh to me, and saith he, ' Brocky,' he saith—that's a name he calleth me, Brocky, friendly like, though he warn't no friend o' mine that I know of—Well, he saith, ' Brocky, I know of so pretty a nest of Rabbits as a Badger could wish to see. I can't dig mun out,' he saith, ' but you can. Oh ! what I would give to be able to dig like you, Brocky ! ' he saith. ' Come 'long wi' me, and I'll show 'ee.' Well, now I'll tell 'ee which way we went."

" No, never mind that," said the Hind, " we mustn't keep you, you know."

" Aw ! " said the Badger, " well, we come to the bury, and wonderful sweet they rabbits did smell, sure enough. ' Now,' he saith, ' I'll leave 'ee.' And I digged the rabbits out ; I forget how many there was—eight or nine I think—I ate mun all up, I know, and very sweet they was, I won't deny that. And then I went 'oom, but bless your life, when I got there I couldn't go into mun. Oh! 'twas terrible sure enough; 'twas more than my poor nose could stand. And the old Fox he looketh out and saith, ' 'Tis wonderful kind of you, Brocky,' he saith, ' to give me your house. Mrs. Vicky liketh it wonderful, she doth. Ah! I wish I could dig like you, Brocky,' he saith. And he's taken my house, and here I be. 'Tisn't right; 'tisn't rasonable."

And he waddled away growling out, " 'Tisn't rasonable," for, being a Devonshire Badger, he was of course fond of long words, though he might not always understand their meaning. And the Calf could hardly help laughing as he saw the poor, stupid old fellow blundering on his way.

But if he fared ill, the Vixen and her Cubs fared well enough. The Cubs grew so fast that they began to look after themselves, and they were often to be seen wandering about the wood, grubbing after beetles and gobbling up the fallen berries. And the Calf grew also, for he was now four months old, you must remember; and of all the months in his life, those first four were, I suspect, the happiest.

CHAPTER IV

EARLY one morning, it must have been almost the last week in September, the peace of the oak-coppice was disturbed by a terrible clamour. It began with a single deep "Ough, ough, ough!" then another voice chimed in with rather a shriller note, and then another and then another, and then a whole score more joined them in one thundering chorus. And the Hind started to her feet in alarm, and led the Calf out of the wooded valley to the open moor above. There they stood listening; while the whole valley was filled with the tumult, as if a hundred demons had been let loose into it. Now and again it ceased for a moment, and all was still; then it began again with "Ough, ough, ough!"; and it was hard to say exactly where the sound came from, for one side of the valley said it would hold it no longer, and tossed it over to the other, and the other said it wouldn't hold it either and tossed it back, so that the

noise kept hovering between the two in the most
bewildering way. But after a short time the clamour
drew nearer to the Hind and Calf, and presently out
came one of the Fox-cubs, with his tongue lolling
and his back crooked, looking desperately weary and
woe-begone. He went on for a little distance, as if
to go away over the moor, but soon stopped and flung
back with desperation into the covert. And the
Hind trotted gently away, anxious but not alarmed.
"They are not after us, my son, I think," she said.
Then the noise drew closer and closer, and out
bounded a whole pack of hounds, with bristles erect
and gleaming eyes, throwing their tongues furiously
on the line of the Cub. They flashed over the scent
for fifty yards, still yelling with all their might, and
then they fell silent and spread out in all directions.
Presently they recovered the line of the Cub, and
turned back into the covert yelling louder than ever;
but meanwhile two wild puppies had crossed the
scent of the Hind and Calf and started after them as
fast as they could run.

Then the Hind turned and fled and the Calf with
her, as he had never fled before; but his poor little legs
began speedily to tire, and he could not have held out
for much longer, when suddenly he found himself

poked down quick as thought by his mother's nose into
a tuft of fern. "Lie still, my son, till I come back,"
she whispered; and so she left him. And there he
lay panting, while the voices of the puppies came
closer and closer to his hiding-place; but he never
moved, for his mother had bid him lie still. Then
they rushed past him with a wild cry, for his mother
had waited to lead them after herself; and their
voices died away, and all was silent. Presently he
heard a dull sound, coming drum, drum, drum,
louder and louder and louder; and then the earth
began to shake, and a huge dark body seemed to be
coming almost on to the top of him, but suddenly
swerved aside just in time, and left him unharmed.
Then the drumming died away, and after a time he
heard a dismal yelping such as he had once heard
before; but he did not know that it was a man and
horse that had nearly galloped on to the top of him,
and would have galloped quite on the top of him if
the horse had not shied, nor that the man had given
the puppies a thrashing for running a deer when
they had been told to run a fox.

He was beginning to hope that his mother would
soon come back, when he heard two voices quite
unlike any that he had ever heard before, and saw

riding towards him two people. One was a man with fair hair and blue eyes, and a face burned brown by the sun, and the other a girl, a year or there-about younger than the man. She, too, had bright blue eyes, and very fair hair, and a very pretty face —at least the man seemed to think so, for he was always looking at it—though of course the Calf, having never seen such creatures before, could not judge if they were pretty or ugly. They came on till they were only at a little distance from him, and the man pulled up and, pointing to him, said very low, "Look." And the girl whispered, " What a little duck ! I wish I could take him home with me." But the man said, " No, no, no. His mother will come and take him home presently, and the sooner we leave him alone the better she will be pleased." So they rode away, and he could hear them talking as they rode, for they seemed to have a great deal to say to each other. But what they talked about, and how they came to stay alone on the hill when the hounds were running down in the valley, is more than I can tell you.

Before very long his mother came back to him, and you may guess how glad he was to see her, and how she rejoiced to see him. After looking round to see that all was quiet, she led him away over the heather, and then down a very steep hill-side among stunted gorse and loose stones, hot and burning from the sun. "See, my son," she said, "this is the first time that you have been chased by hounds, but I fear that it may not be the last. Now, remember, no hound can run fast over this short gorse, for his feet are soft; while we do not mind it, for our feet are hard. And these loose stones are almost better for us than the gorse, for our scent hardly lies on them and they hurt a hound's feet almost as much as the gorse." So they went to the bottom of the hill, and there was a peat-stream singing its song; but all that the Calf could hear of it was this:—

> *I carry no scent, come here, come here;*
> *I am the friend of the wild Red-Deer.*

The Hind led him up a shallow for a little way, and then she jumped out on to the opposite bank and followed it upwards for a little way, and then she jumped into the water again and went down for a full hundred yards till they came to a comfortable shady spot, where they both left the water and lay down together. "Now, my son," she said, "here is another little lesson for you to learn. The song of the water is true; it carries no scent, and no hound can follow us in it unless he can see us. But a hound will always try the bank to find out where we have left the water; if we enter it up the stream he will try upward, and if we enter it down the stream he will try downward. So always, if you have time, try to make them work upward when you mean to go down, and downward when you mean to go up, as I have shown you to-day." And like a wise little fellow he took care to remember what she taught him.

They lay there together till the sun began to fall low, and then they rose and went down to the water to cross it. And there what should they see but a large shoal of little Fish with bright red spots, and bands, like the marks of a finger, striping their sides from gills to tail; for the stream was so clear that they could distinguish every mark upon them. The little Fish seemed to be very anxious about something, for they kept darting about, now spreading out and now all coming together again; and the Calf could hear them whispering, " Shall we ask her ? Shall we, shall we ? " And at last one little Fish rose, with a little splash, and said in a watery little voice :

" Oh ! please can you tell us how far it is to the sea ? "

"Why, my little fellow," said the Hind, "surely it isn't time for you to go to sea yet?"

"Oh, no," said the little Salmon, "for we haven't got our silver jackets yet. But we are *so* looking forward to it. Will our silver jackets come soon, do you think?"

"Not just yet, I expect," said the Hind kindly; "you must have patience, you know, for a little time, only for a little time."

"Oh," said the little Salmon, in a sadly disappointed tone; and the whole shoal began to move away, but almost directly came back and began popping up to the surface of the water by dozens, saying, "Thank you," "thank you," "thank you." For little Salmon are not only very well-bred but very well-mannered besides, which all well-bred creatures ought to be, but unfortunately very often are not.

So they left the little Salmon, and went their way to the cliffs that overhang the sea, where they made their home in a great plantation of Scotch firs, so closely cropped by wind and salt that they cannot grow up into trees but run along the ground almost like ivy. And let me warn you, by the way, when you ride fast through these stunted plantations, as I

hope you may many times, to grip your saddle tight
with your legs and keep your toes turned in, or you
may find yourself on the ground on the broad of your
back; which will not hurt you in the least, but may
lose you your start in a good run.   Well, here they
lay, and very much the Calf liked his new home;
but they had not been there for three days when one
morning they heard faint sounds of a great trampling
of hoofs.   It lasted for a long time, but they lay
quite still, though the Hind was very uneasy.   Then
suddenly they heard the voice of hounds rise from
the coverts on the cliff below them, and a man
screaming at the top of his voice.   The sounds came
nearer, and then there was a great clatter of branches,
and the great Stag, whom they had known on the
moor, came bounding leisurely through the thicket.
His head was thrown back and his mouth wide open;
and very proud and very terrible he looked as he
cantered straight up to them.   He jerked his head
impatiently at them, and said very sternly, "Off with
you! quick!"   And the Hind jumped up in terror
and the Calf with her; and as they ran off they
could see the old Stag lie down in their place with
his great horns laid back on his shoulders, and his
chin pressed tight to the ground.

But they had no time to lose, for the hounds were coming closer; so they bustled for a little way through the thicket, and then the Hind led the Calf into a path, because of course his little legs could not keep pace with hers in the tangle of the plantation. Thus they ran on for a little way, till they heard the sound of a horse coming towards them, when they turned into the thicket again and lay down. And presently a man in a red coat came trotting by with his eyes fixed on the ground, and meeting the hounds stopped them at once. Then he pulled out a horn, blew one single note, and trotted away with the hounds, just three couple of them, at his heels.

But the Hind and Calf lay still; and presently they heard two more horses coming gently along the path, and two human voices chattering very fast. And who should ride by but the pretty girl whom he had seen looking at him a few days before! A man was riding with her, but not the man that he had seen with her before, for this one was dark, and besides he was rather older; but as they passed they saw her smile at him, and open her pretty eyes at him, in a way that seemed to please him very well.

So they rode on till their chattering could be heard no more; and then another man came riding by on a grey horse, quite alone, whom the Calf recognised as the fair man that had been with the girl when first he saw her ; and very doleful and miserable he seemed to be. For he stopped on the path opposite to them, looking down at the ground with a troubled face, and kept flicking savagely at the heather with his whip, till at last he flicked his poor horse on the nose by mistake, and was obliged to pat him and tell him how sorry he was. How long he might have stopped there no one knows ; but all of a sudden the Hind and Calf heard a wild sound of men hallooing, and the horn sounding in quick, continuous notes. Then the man's face brightened up directly, and he caught hold of the grey horse by the head and galloped off as fast as he could go.

Directly after this, the Deer heard a mighty rush of hoofs all hastening to the same spot, the sound growing gradually fainter and fainter until all was still. But they lay fast till a white Sea-gull flew high over their heads chirping out, "They're gone, they're gone," in a doleful voice; not, you know, because he was sorry that all the men and horses were gone, but because Sea-gulls, for some reason, can never say anything cheerfully. And then the Hind arose and led the Calf cautiously out of the plantation to the open moor; and as they went they saw a long string of horses, reaching for two or three miles, toiling painfully one after the other; while far ahead the hounds, like white specks, kept creeping on and on and on, with a larger speck close to them which could be nothing else than a grey horse. So the Hind led the Calf on to a quiet combe, and there they lay down in peace.

And when the sun began to sink they saw, far away, the hounds and a very few horses with them, returning slowly and wearily home. But presently they were startled by voices much closer to them, and they saw the fair man on the grey horse and the pretty girl, riding side by side. The Hind was a little alarmed at first, but there was no occasion for it ; for the pair were riding very close together, so close that his hand was on her horse's neck, and they seemed to be far too much occupied with each other to think of anything else. So they passed on ; and after they were gone there came a loose horse, saddled and bridled, but covered all over with mire, and with a stirrup missing from the saddle.

And presently he lay down and rolled over and over till the girths parted with a crack and left the saddle on the ground; then he got up, hung up one hind-leg in the reins, and kicked himself free; then he lay down again, and rubbed his cheeks against the heather until he had forced the bridle over his head; then he gave himself a great shake to make quite sure that he had got rid of everything, and at last he went down to the water and drank, and wandered off grazing as happy as could be.

Last of all came a man tramping wearily over the heather, with a stirrup in his hand; but the Calf hardly recognised him as the dark man whom he had seen in the morning, for his hat was crushed in, and his clothes caked with mire from head to foot. And he toiled on, looking round him on all sides, till he caught his foot in a tussock of grass, and fell on his nose; and what he said when he got up I don't know, though I might guess, for he looked very cross.

So he too passed out of sight, and the sun went down, and the mist stole over the face of the moor, and the Hind and Calf were left alone with the music of the flowing water to sing them to sleep. But they never saw that old Stag again.

CHAPTER V

AND now the grass of the forest turned fast from green to yellow, the blossom faded off the heather, and the leaves of the woods turned to gold and to russet and to brown, and fluttered down to the kind earth which had raised them up in the spring. The nights too grew chillier and chillier; but the Hind and Calf did not mind that, for their coats only grew the thicker and warmer to protect them. But what was far more terrible was the hideous roaring that continued all night long in all quarters of the moor. It was some days before the Calf found out what it was, for his mother seemed always dreadfully frightened unless he were well hidden away. But once when she had left him for a short time snugly tucked away on a combe's side, he saw a great Stag come down the combe driving a little herd of half a dozen Hinds before him. The Calf was astonished at the sight of him, for the Stag was quite different now from any that he had seen in the summer. The glossy coat was gone, and the great round body was lean, ragged, and tucked up, and stained with half-dried mud. His neck again was twice its usual size and looked still bigger under its great shaggy mane; and his face was not noble and calm, but fierce and restless and furrowed by two deep dark lines, so that altogether he was a most disreputable-looking old fellow.

Presently he stopped at a little boggy spot by the water's side; and there he reared up, and plunging his great antlers into the ground he tore it up, and sent the black mire flying over his head. Then he threw himself down into the bog and rolled in it and wallowed in it, churning it up with horn and hoof, like a thing possessed. At last he got up, all dripping and black, and stretching out his great neck, till the hair of his mane hung straight and lank with the black drops running from it, he roared and roared again with a voice so terrible and unearthly that the Calf in his hiding-place shook with fright. And no wonder, for I think that even you will be startled the first time that you hear a big Stag belling.

Very soon an answering roar came from a dis-

tance, and another Stag, as thin and fierce-looking as
the first, but not quite so big, came belling up the
combe. And the great Stag left the Hinds and went
forward to meet him, looking very stately and grand.
For he walked on tip-toe, loftily and slowly, with his
head thrown back, and his chin high in air, while his
eyes rolled with rage, and his breath spurted forward
in jets of steam through the cold, damp air, as he
snorted defiance. Then presently both Stags dropped
their heads and made for each other; and they
fought with locked horns, shoving and straining and
struggling, backward and forward and round and
round, till the smaller Stag could fight no longer but
turned and fled limping away, with the blood flowing
from a deep thrust in his flank. Then the great Stag
threw up his head and belled again with triumph,
and huddling the Hinds together once more, he drove
them on before him.

For three weeks and more this roaring and fighting continued; for Deer, you must know, put all the
quarrelling of the year into a single month; which
sounds like a curious arrangement, but may after all
be better than that of certain other creatures, which
fight the whole year round. All this while the
Calf's mother kept him carefully out of the way of

stags; but none the less he had visitors. For one day a little brown bird with a long beak came flapping rather crookedly up the combe as if uncertain whither to go next, and then suddenly making up her mind, came down and lighted in front of the Calf's very nose. He was a little astonished, but his mother gave the little bird her kindest glance and said:

"Welcome back to Exmoor, Mistress Woodcock. How have you fared this dry summer, and what passage had you over the sea?"

And the little bird answered with somewhat of a foreign accent and in rather a sad voice, "I am safe and sound, my lady Hind, for we had good weather; but there were a few that started before me, and are not yet come, and I greatly fear that they were blown into the sea by a storm. And the summer was so dry that many springs failed, and many times I had to catch up my chicks and carry them one by one to new feeding-grounds over the pine-forests and across the blue fiords. Ah! you think much of Exmoor, but you have never seen Norway, where your highest hills would be lost among our mountains, and your broadest streams a trickle beside our rivers. We do not duck and dive there, my lady Hind; we fly high and straight, and chirp for joy in our flight, but in this grey England we have not the heart to chirp." And rising with a *flip flap* of her wings she flew silently and sadly away.

At length one day the Hind said: "Son, it is time for you to see some more of your relations." So they set out together; and as they went they passed by all the places which the Calf had known so well when he was but a few weeks old. But they saw no deer, and when they looked about for the Greyhen they could not see her either; nor would they have heard anything of them, if the Hind had not be-thought her of going to see old Bunny. And they found her as usual sitting in front of her bury, looking quite happy and comfortable, with her head a little on one side.

" Why, my lady, you'm quite a stranger," she said when they greeted her. " Lady Yeld and Lady Ruddy was axing for 'ee but two days agone, and says they, ' Tell her we'm going to Dunkery'; and that's where you'm going, I reckon, my lady. And Lady Ruddy's Calf is grown wonderful, and a sweet, pretty little thing she is, but not so pretty as yours, my lady. Look to mun, now, in his little brown coat, a proper little buty. 'Tis just what I was

saying to the old Greyhen—let's see, what day was
it?—well, I don't rightly mind the day, but says I,
' Neighbour, her ladyship's little son—' "

"But where is the Greyhen gone, Bunny?" said
the Hind.

"Well, I don't rightly know, my lady," answered
Bunny. "She comed to me a good whiles back, and
she saith, ' Neighbour, the men's been here shooting
again, and I shall go.' But it was a good whiles
back; I think 'twas when I was rearing my fourth
family,—for I have had two more families since I
seed your ladyship last, aye, and fine ones too. And
I've got a new mate, my lady. You mind my Bucky,
my lady, he that was always lying out—well, he
went out one day and he never comed home again, and
I reckon the weasels catched mun. He was a good
mate was the old Bucky, but he was the half of a
fule—that I should say so—wouldn't never mind
what I told mun. And what was I to do, my lady?
So I tooked another mate. 'Twas not a long courting,
for he comes to me, and, saith he—"

"But where did you say that the Greyhen was
gone?" asked the Hind, kindly.

"I think Clog's Down was the place that she
said, my lady. But, bless your life, she'll come back

here, you may depend. For she's getting up an old bird, my lady,—"

"And there's no place like home, Bunny," said the Hind.

"Aye," said Bunny, "and that's just what I was saying only yesterday to the old Woodcock when she comed telling to me about Norway. 'Get along with 'ee and your Norwayses,' I says ; 'isn't Exmoor good enough for 'ee? Many's the fine brood or Woodcocks that I've seen reared on Exmoor, without never crossing the sea. Look at me,' I says ; '*I* don't go crossing the sea, and look to the broods I've reared.' And now, let me think, how many broods is it?—"

But she took such a long time counting, that, though the Hind was longing to hear, they were obliged to bid her good-day and go on their way. Besides, to tell truth, the Calf was so much pleased when he heard her speak of his brown coat that he was dying to find some one to whom he could show it. And in the very first water that they crossed he saw the little Salmon come hurrying towards them, and called out to them, " Come and look at my brown coat."

But they answered all together, " Come and look

at our silver jackets. We've got our silver jackets, we've got our silver jackets! And the rain will come down to-night, and we'll be off to the sea to-morrow—hurrah!" And they leaped out of the water and turned head over tail with joy, taking no more notice of the Calf's brown coat than if it had been a rag of green weed.

So he passed on with his mother, a little disappointed, and away from the yellow grass of the forest to the brown heather of Dunkery. And there the heath was full of great stones, unlike any ground that he had ever travelled over before, so that he had to be careful at first how he trod. But he soon found that it was easy enough for him after he had gone a little distance ; and his mother led him slowly so that he should have time to learn his way. So on they went to the very top of the ridge, and there where the heather and grass grow tuft by tuft among the brown turf-pits, in the heart of the bog, they found a herd of Deer. Such a number of them there were as he had never dreamed of. Great Stags, with three and four on top, like those that he had seen fighting, were lying down, four and five together, in perfect peace, and younger Stags with lighter heads and fewer points, and Two-year-olds, proud as Punch of their first brow-antlers, and Prickets, even prouder of their first spires than the Two-year-olds, and a score or more of Hinds, nearly all of them with Calves at foot; and standing sentry over all was old Aunt Yeld.

"Come along, my dears," she said patronisingly, "the more the merrier. You'll find a few dry beds still empty in the wet ground, where Ruddy and her Calf are lying; but I warn you that you will have to move before nightfall."

So they went, and found Ruddy and her Calf and lay down by them, for you may be sure that mothers and Calves had a great deal to say to each other. But as the evening began to close they heard a faint, low, continuous hum from the westward, and all the hinds with one accord left the bog, and went down into a deep, snug, sheltered combe, clothed thick with dwarf oak-coppice, while the stags went to their own chosen hiding-places. Soon the hum grew louder and louder, and presently the rain began to fall in heavy drops, as the little Salmon had foretold (though how they could foretell it, I know no more than you); and then the hum changed to a roar as the Westerly Gale came up in all his might and swept across the moor. And presently an old Dog-Fox came in and shook himself and lay down

not far from them on one side, and a Hare came in
and crouched close to them on the other, and little
birds driven from their own roosting-places flew
trembling into the branches above them; but not one
dared to speak except in a whisper, and then only to
say, "What a terrible night!" For all night long
the gale roared furiously over their heads and the
rain and scud flew screaming before it; and once
they heard something whistle over their heads, crying
wildly in a voice not unlike a sea-gull's, "Mercy,
mercy, mercy!" Then the little stream below them
in the combe began to swell and pour down fuller
and fuller; and all round the hill a score of other
little streams swelled likewise, and came tearing down
the hill, adding their roar to the roar of the gale; so
you may be sure that the Salmon had a fine flood to
carry them down to the sea.

When the Deer moved out in the morning they
found the rain and wind raging as furiously as ever,
and the air full of salt from the spray of the sea;
and a few hundred yards to leeward of the combe
they came upon a little sooty Sea-bird, quite a
stranger to them, lying gasping on the ground. The
poor little fellow could only say, "Mercy, mercy,
where is the sea, where is the sea? Where are my

brother Petrels ? " Then he flapped one little wing
feebly, for the other had been dashed by the gale
against a branch and broken, and gasped once more
and lay quite still; nor, though the deer gazed at
him for long, did he ever speak or move again. So
when they had fed, the deer moved back to the
shelter of the combe and lay down there once more;
and as the morning grew the rain ceased, though the
wind blew nearly as hard as ever. But it was still
a good hour before noon when the Hare suddenly
jumped up and stole out of the combe. A minute
after her the Fox stood up, listened for a moment,
and stole out likewise, and almost directly after him
the deer all sprang to their feet; for they heard the
deep note of the hounds and saw their white bodies
dashing into the combe full of eagerness and fire.
And if any one tells you that it is incredible that Deer,
Fox, and Hare should all be lying together as I have
said, you may tell him from me that I saw them
with my own eyes leave the combe one after another
by the same path, on just such a wild morning as I
have described.

The deer moved quickly on to the hill and
began to run away together; but presently Aunt
Yeld, and Ruddy and her Calf, and our Hind and

her Calf separated from the rest, and went away at
a steady pace, for as old Aunt Yeld said, "No hound
can travel fast over Dunkery stones." And, indeed,
so fond was the old lady of these stones that, when
she got to the edge of them, she turned back over
them again and took Ruddy with her. But our
Hind and her Calf moved away a mile or two
towards the forest, and finding no hounds in chase of
them stopped and rested.

But after half an hour or more Aunt Yeld came
galloping up to them alone, very anxious though not
the least tired, and said, "I can't shake them off.
Come along quick!" Then they found that the
hounds were hard at their heels, and away they went,
in the teeth of the gale, at their best pace. And the
Calf kept up bravely, for he was growing strong, but
they were pressed so hard that presently Aunt
Yeld left them and turned off by herself. Then
by bad luck some of the hounds forsook her
line for that of his mother and himself, and drove
them so fast that for the first time in their lives
they were obliged to part company, and he was
left quite alone. So on he ran by himself till he
came to a familiar little peat-stream, which was
boiling down over the stones like a torrent of brown

ale ; and in he jumped and ran down, splashing himself all over. Before he had gone down it fifty yards
he felt so much refreshed that he quite plucked up
heart, so he followed the water till it joined a far
bigger stream, crossed the larger stream, climbed up
almost to the top of the opposite side of the combe,
and lay down.

And when he had lain there for more than an
hour he saw Aunt Yeld coming down to the water
two or three hundred yards above the place where he
lay, with her neck bowed and her grey body black
with sweat, looking piteously tired and weak. She
jumped straight into the flooded water and came
plunging down ; and only a few minutes behind her
came the hounds. The moment that they reached
the water some of them leaped in and swam to the
other side, and they came bounding down both banks,
searching diligently as they ran. Then he saw Aunt
Yeld stop in a deep pool, and sink her whole body
under the water, leaving nothing but her head above
it. She had chosen her place cunningly, where the
bank was hollowed out and the water was overhung
by a little thorn bush that almost hid her head from
view. And he watched the hounds try down and
down ; and he now saw that two horsemen were

coming down the combe's side after them, the men
bending low over their saddles, hardly able to face
the gale, and the horses with staring eyes and heaving
flanks, almost as much distressed as Aunt Yeld herself.
The men seemed to be encouraging the hounds,
though in the howling of the wind he could hear
nothing.

But the pack tried down and down by themselves,
till at last they came to the place where Aunt Yeld
was lying; and there two of them stopped as if
puzzled; but she only sank her head a little deeper
in the water and lay as still as death, with her ears
pressed back tight upon her neck. Then at last the
hounds passed on, though they were loth to leave
the spot, and followed the bank down below her.
But presently the Calf became aware, to his terror,
that some of them were pausing at the place where he
himself had left the water, and, what was more, were
unwilling to leave it. And then a great black and
tan hound carried the line very, very slowly a few
yards away from the bank up the side of the combe,
and said, " Ough ! " and the hounds on the opposite
side of the stream no sooner heard him than they
jumped in and swam across to him; so that in half a
minute every one of them was working slowly up

towards his hiding-place. He was so much terrified that he hardly knew whether to lie still or to fly ; but presently the black and tan hound said " Ough ! " once more with such a full, deep, awful note that he could stand it no longer, but jumped up at once and bounded up over the hill.

And then every hound threw up his head and yelled in a way which brought his heart into his mouth, but he was soon out of their view over the crest of the hill, and turning round set his head backward for Dunkery. And as he went he saw the horsemen come struggling up the hill, trying to call the hounds off, but unable to catch them. But he soon felt that he had not the strength to carry him to Dunkery, so he swung round again with the gale in his face, and then by great good luck he caught the wind of other deer, and running on found that it was Ruddy and her Calf.

By the time that he had joined them the men had stopped the hounds, and were taking them back to try down the water again after Aunt Yeld. But you may be sure that Aunt Yeld had not waited for them. On the contrary, she had made the best of her time, for she had run up the big water again, and turned from it up a smaller stream, and having run up that, was lying down in the fervent hope that she was safe.

And safe she was; for as luck would have it the wind backed to the south-east and began blowing harder than ever, with torrents of rain, so that after another hour the Calf saw horsemen and hounds travelling slowly and wearily home, as drenched and draggled and miserable as a deer could wish to see them. And a little later his mother came and found him, and though she too was terribly tired, she cared nothing about herself in the joy of seeing him. Then after a time Aunt Yeld came up too and joined them, and quite forgetting that it was not at all like a stag to be soft-hearted, she came up to him and fondled him, and said, " My brave little fellow, you have saved my life to-day." So they made their way to the nearest shelter and curled up together to keep each other warm, banishing all thought of the day's adventures in their joy that they were safe.

CHAPTER VI

AFTER this they were left in peace for a short time, but week after week the hounds came to Dunkery or to the forest, and though the Deer were not always obliged to run their hardest, yet it was seldom that they had not to fly, at any rate for a time, for their lives. So after a few weeks the Hind led the Calf back to the wood where they had made the acquaintance of the Vixen and the Badger; and there they were left alone. For there came a hard frost which covered the moor with white rime, and, though it sometimes sent them far afield for food, still saved them from annoyance by hounds. But the poor Blackbirds and Thrushes suffered much, for they were weak for want of food; and often the Calf would see them in the hedges crawling over the dead leaves, unable to fly. And then the old Vixen would come round (for she was still there, though all her Cubs were scattered), and pick up the poor struggling little birds, and make what meal she could of them, though there was little left of them but skin and bone ; for she too was ravenous with hunger.

But at last the frost broke up and the warm rain came, and the days grew longer, and the sun gathered strength. So after a time they began to wander over the skirt of the moor again, and thus one day they saw a curious sight. For in the midst of the heather stood a number of Greyhens, looking very sober, and modest and respectable, and round them, in a ring worn bare by the trampling of their feet, a number of Blackcocks were dancing like mad creatures, with their beautiful plumage fluffed out and their wings half spread, to show what handsome fellows they were. While they watched them one splendid old Cock came waltzing slowly round, with his feathers all gleaming in the chill sunshine, and all the time looking out of the corner of his eye at one of the Hens. And as generally happens when people look one way and go another, particularly if they chance to be waltzing, he ran full against another Cock, who was just in front of him, and nearly knocked him over. Whereupon he asked the other Cock very angrily, " Now then, where be coming to ? "

But the other answered quite as angrily: " If you come knacking agin me again like that, you old dumphead, I'll spoil your plumes for 'ee, I will."

Then the old bird shook out all his feathers in a towering passion, and said: " *You* spoil my plumes, you little, miser'ble, dirty-jacketed roog! You spoil my plumes! If you dare to come anigh me, I'll give 'ee such a dressing as you won't get over this side midsummer. I'll teach 'ee to call me dump-head ! "

But the other was quite as quarrelsome, and answered very rudely: " You give me a dressing? I'd like to see 'ee try it. Git out of the way, and don't come here telling of your dressings. I bean't afeard to call 'ee dumphead. Now then, dumphead, dumphead, dumphead ! "

And with that they flew at each other, and pecked and scratched and ruffled, and beat each other with their wings, till all the ground was covered with their feathers. And all the time the Greyhens kept whispering to each other, " He's down—no, he's up—no, he's down again. He's too strong for

mun. Dear, dear, but the old bird's sarving mun
bad!" And so he was, for after a hard fight the old
Cock came back breathless and crowed with triumph,
screaming, "Now, then, who's the better bird?"

And the Greyhens answered in chorus: "Why,
you be, my dear. Ah! you'm a rare bird, sure
enough. Get your breath, my dear, for 'tis sweetly
pretty to see 'ee dance."

So the Deer left them dancing and fighting, and
making their way over the moor again to Dunkery,
went down into Horner Wood. And they found
the wood quiet and peaceful as if no hound had
ever been near it; and above their heads the oak-
buds were swelled and ripe almost to bursting, while
under their feet was a carpet of glossy green and
blue, picked out with stars of pale yellow, for the
bluebells and primroses had thrust their heads
through the dead leaves to welcome the spring.
The gorse, too, was flaming with yellow blossom,
the thorns were gay in their new green leaves, and
the bracken was thrusting up its green coils,
impatient to uncurl and make a shelter for the
deer.

They rarely saw an old stag, though they met
a young one or two, and they did not even see

many hinds, though they frequently met and talked to Ruddy. And the Calf now became better friends than ever with Ruddy's daughter, for, having both of them seen a great deal of the world after a life of one whole year, they had plenty to talk about. One day she told him, as a great secret, that her mother had promised her a little brother before many months should be past; but all that he did was to make her promise that she would still like him best. And the truth is that he began to think himself rather too fine a fellow to be interested in calves when there were older male deer to associate with. For as soon as the ash began to sprout, all the male deer in Horner formed clubs to go and eat the young shoots, for there is nothing that they love so much to eat; and he of course went among them and nibbled away as greedily as any, though not being the biggest deer he did not of course get the biggest share.

Besides, not long after the ash was in leaf, he began to feel rather a pain in his head; and although a headache is not generally a pleasant thing, yet this was so slight and at the same time so interesting, that he did not much mind it. For on each side of the crown of his head there appeared a little swelling, very hot and tender, which grew into a little knob of black velvet, and which he thought very handsome, though you and I perhaps might not think so. But he was so proud of it that he always looked at it in the water, when he went down to drink of an evening, to see how it was growing. And the best of it was, that not one of the big stags now had much more on their heads than he had, for they had lost their horns, and were looking very foolish with their great necks and manes and nothing to carry on them. He saw the big stags so very seldom now that he could hardly find an opportunity of asking them what had happened; and when at last he got a chance of putting the question to a huge old fellow, whom he came upon one day with his mouth full of ivy, he was in such a hurry that I am afraid he must have seemed inquisitive. For the old Stag stared at him for a minute with the ivy sticking out of his lips, and then said very gruffly, " Go away, and mind your own business. Little calves should be seen and not heard." And our Deer was so much vexed at being called a little Calf, whereas he was really a Pricket, that he slunk away down to the water to have a look at his velvet; but it was getting on so beautifully

that he felt quite comforted, and was glad that,
although the Stag had been so unkind, he had
not said, "You're another," or something rude
and disrespectful of that kind, which would have
been most unbecoming in a Red-Deer.

A few days later the matter was partly explained
to him. For early one morning when he was out at
feed in a growing corn-field with a number of young
male deer, a four-year-old came galloping up the
hedge trough with a sheep-dog racing after him.
The four-year-old was in such a flurry that he jumped
the fence at the corner of the field without noticing
an overhanging branch, and thump! down fell both of
his horns on one side of the hedge, while he galloped
on, leaving them behind him, on the other. The
rest of the deer also went off in a hurry, you may be
sure, after such a scare, for they did not expect a
sheep-dog to be out so early; and, indeed, it is quite
possible that the sheep-dog had no business to be out.
His mother looked very grave when our Pricket told
her about it; and that very night they set out across
the moor, pointing straight for the covert where
they had hidden themselves during the last summer.

And there they found all their old friends; for
the Badger had dug himself a new earth and was

quite happy, and the Vixen had found his old house so convenient that she had turned it into a nursery ; and, as they passed, three little Cubs poked their heads out of one of the holes, and winked at them like so many little vulgar boys. But on the very day after they arrived they heard loud yapping, as of a little dog, about the earth, and crossing to the other side of the valley, they could faintly hear men's voices and the constant clink of iron against stones. And when night came and they ventured to come nearer, they found the old Vixen running about like one distracted, crying for her Cubs ; for the earth was all harried and destroyed, and there could be no doubt that the men had dug the Cubs out and taken them away. And the wailings of the poor old Vixen were so distressing that they left the wood and turned up again over the moor.

Soon they began to pass over strange ground, which rose higher and higher before them. The little streams grew more plentiful, coming down from every side in deep clefts which they had dug through the turf to hasten their journey to the sea ; the ground beneath their feet became softer and softer, though it was never so ill-mannered as to give way under their light step, and the water dripped in-

cessantly down from the ragged edges of the turf
above the clefts. But they went on higher and
higher, till at last they stood on a dreary waste of
rough grass, and miry pools, and turf-pits blanched
by the white bog-flower. For they were on the
great ridge whence the rivers of Exmoor take their
source and flow down on all sides to the sea; and
a wild treacherous tract it is. They passed a little
bird no bigger than a thrush, who had his beak
buried so deep in the mire that he could not speak;
and the Hind said, "Good day, Master Snipe. Your
wife and family are well, I hope?" Then the little
bird hastily plucked a long bill out of the ground,
though his mouth was so full of a big worm that he
was obliged to be silent for a minute or two; never-
theless at last he gulped the worm down, washed his
bill in a little pool of water, and piped out, "Very
well, thank you, my lady, half-grown or more."

"You couldn't tell me what there is over the
hill?" asked the Hind.

"Not very well, not to tell your ladyship what
you want to know," said the Snipe, "but you'll find
the old Wild-duck a bit farther on and she'll tell
'ee." And he began routling about in the mire again
with his beak.

So they lay down till evening among the turf-pits, and after travelling a little way farther they reached the very top of the hill and saw a new world. For before them the high land of the moor plunged down into a tangle of smaller hills, cut up by great green banks into innumerable little fields, and seamed and slashed by a hundred wooded valleys. Fifty miles before them the land rose high again and swelled up to the tors of Dartmoor, which stood stately and clear and blue against the sky. But on their right hand the moor seemed to leap at one bound many miles to the sea; and they saw the white line of the surf breaking on Bideford Bar, and beyond it Lundy, firm and solid in mid-sea, and far beyond Lundy the wicked rocky snout of Hartland Point, purple and gaunt beneath the sinking sun.

The Hind looked anxiously at the wooded valleys beneath their feet, wondering which she should take; but presently they heard a loud " Quack, quack, quack," and down she went in the direction of the sound. And there in a pool of a little stream they found an old Duck, very prim and matronly, swimming about with her brood all round her, and tne Mallard with them. Whereupon of course the

Hind stopped in her civil way to ask after her and her little Flappers.

" Why, bless 'ee, my lady, they'm getting 'most too big to be called Flappers," answered the Duck, " and I shall take mun out and down the river to see the world very soon. They do tell me that some ducks takes their broods straight to the big waters, but they must be strange birds, and I don't hold wi' such. 'Twas my Mallard was a-telling me. What was it you told me you saw down the river, my dear ? "

But the old Mallard was shy and silent; he only mumbled out something that they could not hear, and swam away apart. Then the old Duck went on in a whisper : " You see, my lady, he's just a-beginning to change his coat, and very soon he'll be so dingy as I be for a whole month, till his new coat cometh. Every year 'tis the same, and he can't abear it, my lady, for it makes folk think that he's a Duck and no Mallard. Not but that I think that a Duck's coat is beautiful, but a Mallard's more beautiful yet, I can't deny that; but you know, my lady, how vain these husbands be. But he did tell me about they ducks, and I say again I don't hold wi' mun. I reared my brood in the turf-pits and taught mun to swim, and bringed them down the little streams where they couldn't come to no harm till they was big enough to take care of theirselves. And I don't hold with no other way, for I'm not a-going to have my little ducks drownded."

"And is the river quiet?" asked the Hind; "and could we live in the valley?"

"The valley's so quiet as a turf-pit, my lady," said the old Duck, " beautiful great woods for miles down. Surely I've heard tell that your family lived there years agone."

So they took leave of the Ducks, and going down into the strange valley found it as she had said. The woods ran down by the little river for miles ; and though the valley left the moor far behind it, yet there were fields of grass, and corn, and turnips, full of good food whenever they might want it; so they decided to make themselves very comfortable there for the whole summer.

CHAPTER VII

ONE day when they were out at feed our Pricket
caught sight of a little brown bird with a full dozen
of little chicks cheeping all round her; and as he
was always anxious to make new friends he trotted
up to scrape acquaintance with the stranger. But
what was his astonishment when the little bird
fluffed out her wings and flew at him.

"You dare to touch mun," she said furiously,
"you dare to touch mun, and I'll peck out the
eyes of 'ee."

"But, my dear soul," he said, "I won't do you
any harm."

"Oh, beg your pardon," said the little bird, "I
didn't see who it was, and I made sure that it was
one of they sheep-dogs. But I don't mind ever to
have seen one of you here; I thought you belonged
farther down the valley."

"But I come from the moor," he said.

" I ha'n't never been on the moor," said the little bird, " but there's more of 'ee down the valley, at least I think there be, for, begging your honour's pardon, I don't rightly know who you be. Do 'ee want to know the way? Then follow down the river till you'm clear of the woods and then turn up over the fields, till you see another wood, and that will bring 'ee to the place where your friends be. And I beg your honour's pardon for mistaking your honour for a sheep-dog, for I've never seen the like of you before, but they sheep-dogs do worry us poor Partridges terrible."

And she bustled away with her Chicks. But the Pricket was so much excited to hear of other Deer that he entreated his mother to go where the Partridge had told them. And they went just as she had said, over the fields and into the wood that she spoke of, but to their disappointment saw no sign of a deer there. So they passed on through the wood to the valley again, and then they came to a park with the river running through it, and great trees bigger than he had ever seen, beech and oak and lime and chestnut, some in rows and some in clumps, a beautiful expanse of green, all dripping in the morning dew. And there the Pricket saw deer, and

he was so delighted that he ran on by himself to
speak to them; but he was puzzled, for some of them
were black, and some were white, and some were
red, and the greater part were spotted; while not one
was near so big as he was, though many of them had
growing horns as big as his own and bigger. So he
made sure that they must all be calves with some
new description of horn, and going up to the biggest
of them he said rather patronisingly, " Good morning,
my little friend."

But the other turned round and said, " Little
friend! Do you know who I am, sir? I am the
Master-Buck of this park, sir, and I'll trouble you
not to call me your little friend."

" But why don't you come to the woods and on
to the moor ? " said the Pricket, astonished. " I've
never seen you there."

" Did you hear me say that I was the Master-
Buck of this park, sir ? " said the Fallow-Buck, " and
do you know what that means ? I am lord of the
whole of this herd, and master of everything inside
this park-fence. What do I want with woods and
moors, when I have all this beautiful green park for
a kingdom, and all this grass to feed on in the
summer, and hay, sir, hay brought to me in the

winter? Do you get hay brought to you in the winter, sir?"

"Why," broke in the Pricket, "do you mean to say that you can't feed yourself?"

But here the Hind trotted up and fetched her son away. "They are only miserable little tame Fallow-Deer," she said. "You should never have lowered yourself to speak to them."

"No, mother," he answered; "but fancy preferring to live in a wretched little park instead of wandering free through the woods and over the moor! Do let me go back and thrash him."

But when the Fallow-Buck heard this he trotted away as quick as he could; and mother and son went back into the wood. And as they entered it a very handsome bird with a grey back and a rosy breast and bright blue on his wings fluttered over their heads screeching at the top of his voice. "Come in," he said, "please to come right in. But we Jays be put here to scritch when any stranger cometh into the wood, and scritch I must and scritch I shall." And certainly he did, in a most unpleasant tone, for he had been watching a brood of another bird's chicks instead of minding his proper business, and so had missed them when they first came in. So he screeched double to make up for lost time.

Then presently there came towards them another bird, walking very daintily on the ground. He had a green neck and bright red round his eyes, and a coat which shone like burnished copper mixed with burnished gold. He stopped as they came up, and waiting till the Pricket had wandered a little way from his mother, he went up to him and said in a very patronising tone : " Welcome, young sir, welcome to my wood. I have not the pleasure of knowing who you are, but my name I expect is familiar to you. Phasianus Colchicus, ahem—" and he strutted about with great importance. " You have heard of me, no doubt."

" I am afraid not," said the Pricket very civilly. " You see, I come from the moor. But I thought that I saw one or two birds like you as we passed through this wood."

" Like me," said the bird suspiciously ; " are you quite sure that they were like me, like me in every way ? "

" Well," said the Pricket hesitating, " they had pretty white rings round their necks—"

" What ! " broke in the bird, " rings round their

necks, and like me! Oh, the ignorance of young people nowadays. My dear young friend, you have a great deal to learn. Have I a white ring round my neck? No. Well, now I must ask your pardon if I turn my back upon you for one moment." And round he turned very slowly and ceremoniously and stood with his back to the Pricket, who stared at it not knowing what to say.

"Well," said the bird, looking over his shoulder after a time. "You make no remark. Is it possible that you notice nothing? My dear young friend, let me ask you, do you see any green on my back?"

"No," said the Pricket, and honestly he did not.

"So," said the bird very tragically. "Look well at that back, for you will never see such another again, my young friend. I am one of the old English breed, the last of my race, the last of those that, coming centuries ago from the banks of the Phasis, made England their home and were, I may venture to say, her greatest ornament. But now a miserable race of Chinese birds has come in, and go where I will I see nothing but white-ringed necks and hideous green backs. My very children, now no more, took them for wives and husbands, and I alone am left of the old pure breed, the last of the true Pheasants, the last king of this famous wood, the last and the greatest—bless me, what's that? Kok, kok, kok, kok, kok." Thereupon he flipped up into a larch-tree and began at the top of his voice: "You wretched creature, how often have I forbidden you the woods? Go home and catch mice, go home. My dear young friend, let me entreat you to drive that wretch away."

And the Pricket looking round saw a little black and white Cat slinking through the wood close by, a thing he had never seen before and did not at all like the sight of. She took not the least notice of the Pheasant till the Hind trotted down through the covert and said very sternly: "Go home, Pussy, go home. How dare you come out into the woods? Take care, or you'll come to a bad end." And the Cat ran away as fast as she could ; and I may as well say that she did come to a bad end the very next week, for she was caught in a trap and knocked on the head, which last is the fate of all poaching cats sooner or later. So if ever you own a cat, be careful to keep it at home.

"Ah!" said the old Cock-Pheasant, much relieved, as the Cat disappeared. "Is that your mother, my young friend? What an excellent person! You must introduce me some day, but really at this moment I feel quite unfit to leave this tree."

So they left him sitting in the larch tree, not looking at all kingly, and wandered about the wood, finding it very much to their liking; for there was dry ground and wet ground, sunny beds and shady beds, warm places and cool places, and great quiet and repose. And that is why all wild animals love Bremridge Wood and always have loved it.

Now some days after they had made their home there, the Pricket became troubled with a good deal of itching in the velvet on his head. He shook his head violently, but this did no good except to make the velvet fall down in little strips, so at last he picked out a neat little ash-tree and rubbed and scrubbed and frayed till all the velvet fell to the ground, and he was left with a clean little pair of smooth white horns. At this he was so pleased with himself that he must needs go down to the river to look at himself in the water; and after that he could not be satisfied till he had passed through the deer-park to let the Fallow-Deer see him. But here he was a little abashed, for the horns of the Bucks were many of them much bigger than his own, though flat, like your hand, and, as he thought, not nearly so handsome.

The Hind now became restless and inclined to wander, so that they went the round of all the woods in the neighbourhood; and thus it was that one day they came upon ground covered with rhododendrons, and azaleas, and tall pine-trees of a kind that they had never seen before. They would hardly have ventured upon it if they had not heard the quacking of wild-ducks, which led them on till they came upon a little stream. They followed the water downward till they came to a waterfall, where they stopped for a minute in alarm; for at its foot lay the remains of three little ducks quite dead, little more indeed than heaps of wet feathers, only to be recognised by their poor little olive-green beaks. But they still heard quacking below, and going on they presently found a dozen Mallards and Ducks exactly like those that they had seen on the moor, all full-plumed and full-grown.

The Hind went up to them at once, but they took not the least notice of her. She wished them good-morning, but still they took no notice; so then she said in her gentlest voice: " I am afraid that you

have had a dreadful misfortune with your little
Flappers."

Then at last a little Duck turned round and said
very rudely : " Ey ?   What yer s'yin' ? "

" Your little Ducklings which I saw lying dead
by the fall," she said.

" Well," said the Duck still more rudely, " let 'em
lie there. I can't be bothered with 'em. Who asked
you to come poking your nose into our water ? "

The Hind was very angry, for she had never
been spoken to like this, and she remembered how
very differently the Duck had talked to her on the
moor. So instead of leaving these disgraceful little
Ducks alone, which would perhaps have been wiser,
she began to scold them. " What," she said, " do
you mean to say that you let the poor little things
drown for want of proper care ? I never heard of
such a thing. You ought to be ashamed of yourselves."

And then all the Ducks broke out in chorus.
" 'Ow, I s'y, 'ere's an old party come to teach us
'ow to bring up our chicks," said one. " Shall I
just step out and teach your little feller 'ow to
run ? " said another. " Look out, little 'un, or your
'orns will drop off," said a third ; and this annoyed

the Pricket very much, for how could his horns
be dropping off, considering that they were only just
clean of velvet? "The old 'un hasn't got no
'orns," said a fourth; "there's an old Cow in the
next field. Shall I go and borrow a pair for you,
mum? She'll be 'appy to lend 'em, I'm sure."
And they all burst out laughing together, "Quar,
quar, quar, quar!" And I am sorry to say that the
Ducks laughed even louder than the Mallards.

Altogether they were so rude, and impudent, and
vulgar, and odious, that the Deer walked away with
great dignity without saying another word. And
as they went they saw an old grey Fox crouching
down in the rushes by the water-side, as still as
a stone, and quite hidden from view. Then the
Hind turned to warn the Ducks, but she could
hardly utter a word before they all came swimming
down, laughing, "Quar, quar, quar," till she couldn't
hear herself speak. Presently they turned to the
bank, still laughing, and waddled ashore one after
another; when all of a sudden up jumped the Fox,
caught the foremost Mallard by the neck, threw him
over his back, and trotted away laughing in his turn.
And the rest of the ducks flew back to the water
fast enough then, you may be sure, and were sorry

when it was too late that they had been so rude.
But the truth is, that these were not true wild-
ducks, but what are called tame wild-ducks, which
had been bought in Leadenhall Market. And this
accounted for their bad manners, their ugly language,
and their conceit; for like a great many other
creatures that are bred in towns, they thought they
knew everything, whereas in reality they could not
take care of their children nor even of themselves.

The Hind was very much disgusted, and began
to think that she had wandered too far from the
moor, as indeed she had. For on their way back
to Bremridge Wood they were chased by a sheep-
dog, and when they shook him off by jumping a
hedge they found themselves in the middle of a lot
of bullocks, which ran together and galloped after
them and tried to mob them. So they decided to
have no more to do with a country where there were
so many tame things, but to go straight back to the
moor. The Pricket thought that it might be
pleasanter only to move up to their old home in
the woods higher up the valley, but the Hind
was impatient to return to the moor. There was
no one to warn her not to go, and they set out that
very same night.

CHAPTER VIII

THEY were glad to get on to the heather again, and to hear the breeze singing over the moor, and still more glad when they caught the wind of deer and found Aunt Yeld and Ruddy among them. And Lady Ruddy had kept her promise to her little Hind and had given her a little Stag for a brother, a fine little fellow, who was already beginning to shed his white spots and grow his brown coat. But almost directly after they arrived the stags began belling and fighting again, and there was no peace for nearly a month until they had tired themselves out and settled down to live quietly for another year.

Then came a week of sharp frost, which made the ground too hard for the hounds to trouble them; and they really began to think that they might enjoy a quiet winter. Their winter-friends came flocking back to them, the Woodcock arriving one

bright moonlight night with the whole of her own
family and two or three more families besides. They
all settled down above the cliffs where the springs
were kept unfrozen by the sea, and night after night
while the moon lasted the Pricket saw them grubbing in the soft ground with their long bills, and
growing fatter and fatter. But at length one morning the Sea-gulls came in screaming from the sea to
say that the west wind and the rain were coming;
and that very night the frost vanished. Then came
three days of endless grey clouds and mizzling rain,
and then the sun and blue sky returned; and the
Deer moved out of the covert to the open ground to
enjoy St. Martin's summer.

But one day while they were lying in the great
grass tufts in the middle of the wet ground, they
were startled by the approach of horses and hounds;
and they leaped to their feet and made off in all
haste. There were but two hounds after them, but
for all that the Hind and the Pricket were never
more alarmed, for scent as they knew was good, and
the pace at which those two hounds flew after them
was terrible. They had not run above a quarter of
a mile when Aunt Yeld turned off in one direction,
and Ruddy with her Yearling and her Calf in

another; but the hounds let them go where they would, and raced after our Pricket and his mother as if they had been tied to them. They both ran their hardest, but they could not shake off those two hounds, and presently they parted company and fled on, each of them alone. The Pricket made for the cliffs, dashing across the peat-stream without daring to wait for a bath; and as he cantered up the hill towards the refuge that he had chosen, he caught sight of his mother racing over the yellow grass at her topmost speed, and no longer one couple but sixteen couples of hounds racing after her in compact order, not one of them gaining an inch on his neighbour. He saw her gallop up to a gate in a fence and fly over it like an arrow from the bow; and a few minutes after her the hounds also came to the same gate and flew over it likewise, without pausing for an instant, like a handful of white blossoms driven before the wind. Then he turned into the plantation, frightened out of his life, and ran down through them, leaping desperately over the stunted trees and scaring the Woodcocks out of their five wits. And from the plantation he ran down through the oak-woods on the cliff, and from thence to the beach, and then without pausing for a moment he ran straight into the sea and swam out over the waves as only a deer can swim.

The cool water refreshed him; and presently he stopped swimming and turned round, floating quietly on the surface, to see if he was still in danger. But the woods were all silent, and there was no sign of hound or horse on the shore or on the cliff-paths; so after waiting for another quarter of an hour he swam back, and climbed up over the cliff again till he found a stream of fresh water. There he drank a good draught, and passing on came upon a Woodcock, one of those that he had frightened on his way down. The little bird was rather cross at having been disturbed in the middle of her day-dreams, for she said: "What on earth made you come tearing through this wood in that mad way just now? There was nobody hunting you, and nothing of any kind to frighten you. I was in the middle of a delightful dream about Norway, and you quite spoilt it." But he soon soothed her, for woodcocks are easy-going little creatures, and went away and lay down, very much relieved to know that he was unpursued.

When evening came he went away to seek his mother, but he could not find her; and all next day he wandered about asking every deer that he met if they had seen her, but not one could tell him anything. He met Aunt Yeld and Ruddy, but they knew nothing, and he could not ask the hounds who might have told him ; so at last very sorrowfully he gave up searching and made up his mind that she would never come back. And he was right, for she never did come back, and he never saw her again. But, after all, he was old enough to take care of himself, and it was time for him to be making his own way in the world. There were plenty of young deer of his own age to keep him company, and Aunt Yeld and Ruddy's little daughter were still left for old friends. So he settled down comfortably on Dunkery, and by good luck was little troubled the rest of the winter by the hounds.

At last the spring came again and all was peace on the moor. The ash sent forth its green shoots, and as usual all the young male deer came crowding up to eat them ; and our Deer got a larger share this spring, for he was bigger and stronger and could drive the yearlings away. But about the middle of April his head began to ache again, and not only to ache but to irritate him a great deal. It grew worse and worse every day, and one morning it got so troublesome on one side that he gave his head an extra violent shake; and lo and behold! the horn on that side began to totter, and before he could understand what had happened, it fell to the ground. For a minute or two he stood still trembling with pain, for the air struck cold on to the place from which the horn had dropped, and hurt him dreadfully. The pain soon got better, and he went away to hide himself, for he felt very much ashamed at having but one horn. But after a few hours the other side of his head grew as bad as the first, and he was wondering what on earth he should do, when who should come by but another Two-year-old, with both horns still on his head? Now this Two-year-old was rather smaller than our Deer, and rather disliked him because he took a larger share of the ash-sprouts; so thinking that this would be a fine opportunity of taking his revenge, he came at him at once with his head lowered. And our Deer ran away—what else could he do with only one horn against two?—and as he bounded under the oak bushes he knocked his remaining horn against a branch, and thump! off it came as suddenly as the other. But he was able to crow over the Two-year-old in a few days when he too had shed his horns, for our Deer had got the start of him in growing a new pair, and could show two inches of growing velvet where the other could only show one.

So when the autumn came and the velvet began to peel, our Deer found that he had bigger horns than any other deer of his own age, brow, trey and upright, very strong and well-grown; such was his good luck in being an early calf and having had so good a mother. And when another year came (for the years, as you will find out to your cost some day, fly away much faster as one grows older) and he had shed his old horns and grown his new pair, he carried on each horn, brow, bay and trey, with two on top on one side and upright on the other, or nine points in all.

Now towards the end of that summer a great big Stag came up to him and said, "My fine young fellow, it is time that you had nothing more to do with hinds and young things; you must come and be my squire." Now our Deer thought it a great compliment to be noticed by so splendid an old fellow, and went with him gladly enough. The pair of them were constantly together for several weeks; and our Deer found it not unpleasant, for the old Stag knew of all the best feeding grounds, and, though he took all the best of the food for himself, left plenty and to spare for the squire. But it was a shame to see how wasteful this greedy old fellow was. For if they went into a turnip-field he would only take a single bite out of a turnip, worry it out of the ground, and go on to another; while often he would pick up scores of roots and throw them over his head, from mere mischief and pride in the strength of his neck. Again, in the corn-fields he was so dainty that he would not take a whole ear of corn, but would bite off half of it and leave the rest to spoil. Now a hind, as our Deer knew from observing his mother, is far more thrifty. She will take four or five bites out of a turnip before she pulls it out of the ground and leaves it, and she takes the whole of an ear of corn instead of half. But I am sorry to say that our young Deer took example from the great Stag, and soon became as wasteful and mischievous as he was in his feeding; and indeed I never saw nor heard of a stag that had not learned this very bad habit.

The only occasions on which the old Stag did not keep his squire with him was when he went to lie down in the covert for the day after feeding. The lazy old fellow was very particular about his bed, and was aware of all kinds of quiet places in the cliffs, where he knew that the hounds would be unlikely to find him. Or sometimes he would tell his squire to stop for a minute, and then he would make a gigantic bound of twenty feet or more into the midst of some dense thicket, and say to him quietly: "Now I am quite comfortable. Do you go on and lie down by yourself; but don't go too far, and keep to windward of me, so that I can find you if I want you."

And our Deer used to go as he was told, never doubting that all was right; nor was it until late in the autumn that he found out his mistake. For one day while he was lying quietly in the short plantation above the cliffs he heard the familiar cry of hounds, and presently up came the old Stag. He jerked his head at him, just as the other old stag had done when he was a calf, and said very roughly: "Now, then, give me your bed, young fellow, and run instead of me. Look sharp." And our Deer jumped up at once, but he was so angry and astonished at being treated in this way now that he was grown up, that he quite forgot his manners, and said very shortly, "Sha'n't!"

"How dare you? Go on at once," said the

old Stag, quivering with rage and lowering his head, but our Deer lowered his head too and made ready to fight him, though he was but half of his size; and it would have gone hard with him, if just at that moment the hounds had not come up. Then the old Stag threw himself down into his bed with a wicked chuckle; and the hounds made a rush at our Deer and forced him to fly for his life. So there he was, starting alone before the hounds for the first time, and with only a few minutes to make up his mind whither he would go. But what other refuge should he seek but the wood where his mother had led him as a calf? So he left the covert at once and started off gallantly over the heather.

He ran on for five or six miles, for he had been frightened by finding the hounds so close to him when the old Stag drove him out. But after a time he stopped and listened, for he had heard no voice of hounds behind him since he left the covert, and began to doubt whether they were chasing him after all. He pricked his ears intently, and turned round to find if the wind would bear him any scent of his enemies. No! there was not a sign of them. Evidently they were not following him, and he was safe. And this indeed was the case, for, though he did not know it, some men had seen the two deer turn and fight, and, marking the spot where the old Stag had lain down, had brought the hounds back and roused him again. But our Deer was too wary to make sure of his safety without the help of a peat-stream, so he cantered on to the next water and ran up it for a long way till it parted into three or four tiny threads, for he was now on the treacherous, boggy ground where the rivers rise. Then he left the stream and lay down in the tall, rank grass, meaning to wait there till night should come, if he were undisturbed. And lonely though it was, he felt that he was on friendly ground, for all round him the tiny brown streams were singing their song.

Through heather and woodland, through meadow and lea
We flow from the forest [1] away to the sea.
In cloud and in vapour, in mist and in rain
We fly from the sea to the forest again.
Oh! dear is the alder and dearer the fern,
And welcome are kingfisher, ousel and herne,
The swan from the tide-way, the duck from the mere,
But welcome of all is the wild Red-Deer.

---

[1] A forest does not necessarily imply trees. There is not a tree on the forest of Exmoor.

Turn down to the sea, turn up to the hill,
Turn north, turn south, we are with you still.
Though fierce the pursuer, wherever you fly
Our voices will tell where a friend is nigh,
Your thirst to quench, and your strength to stay,
And to wash the scent of your feet away.
Lie down in our midst and know no fear,
For we are the friends of the wild Red-deer.

So there he lay for two hours and more, never doubting but that he was safe, till suddenly to his dismay he thought he heard the voice of a hound, very faint and far away. He lay quite still, and after a time he thought he heard it again; but he could hardly think that the hounds could follow his line after so long a time. He waited and waited, distinctly hearing the sound come nearer, though very slowly, till presently a Blackcock came spinning up to him, whom he recognised as one of the old Greyhen's children. "Beware, my lord, beware," he said; "they'm coming slowly, but they'm a-coming, and I am bound to warn 'ee."

"Are they come to the water?" he asked.

"No," said the Blackcock, "but they'm almost come to it. Bide quiet, and I will keep watch. The old Stag managed to beat the hounds on the cliffs, and as they could not find mun again, the men after waiting a long time laid the pack on your line, and faint though scent was, they have followed it slowly, and follow it yet."

So the Blackcock watched, and saw the hounds puzzling out the scent inch by inch with the greatest difficulty. There were but very few horsemen with them, though the moor was dotted in all directions with a hundred or more of them that had given up the chase and were going away. But a few still stuck to the hounds, which never ceased searching in all directions for the line of the Deer. At last after much puzzling the hounds carried the scent to the water, and there they were brought to their wits' end; but they tried up and up and up with tireless diligence till they came to a place where a huge tuft of grass jutted out high over the water from the bank, and there they stopped.

" Oh, my lord, my lord," whispered the Black-cock, "you didn't never brush the grass as you passed, surely?"

But while he spoke a hound reared up on his hind-legs and thrust his nose into the grass tuft, and said, "Ough! he has passed here;" and the Deer knew the voice as that of the black and tan hound

that had led the way to his hiding-place once before
when he was a calf. Yet he lay still, though
trembling, while the hounds searched on closer and
closer to him, albeit with little to guide them, for
the scent was weak from the water that had run off his
coat when he left the stream. At last, one after another,
they gave up trying, and only the black and tan
hound kept creeping on with his nose on the ground,
till at last he caught the wind of the Deer in his bed,
and stood rigid and stiff with ears erect and nostrils
spread wide. Then the Blackcock rose and flew away
crying, " Fly, my lord, fly," and the Deer jumped up
and bounded off at the top of his speed.

He heard every hound yell with triumph behind
him, but he summoned all his courage, and set his
face to go over the hill to the valley whither the
Wild-Duck had guided him two years before. And
he gained on the hounds, for he was fresh, whereas
they had worked hard and travelled far to hunt him
to his bed. So he cantered on in strength and con-
fidence over bog and turf-pit till he gained the hill-
top, and on down the long slope which led to the
valley, and through the oak-coppice to the water.
Then he jumped in and ran down, while the merry
brown stream danced round him and leaped over his

heated flanks, refreshing him and encouraging him till he felt that he could run on for ever.

He followed it for full two miles and would have followed it still further, when all of a sudden a great Fish like a huge bar of silver came sculling up the stream to him and motioned him back.

"What is it, my Lord Salmon?" he asked.

"There are men on the bank not far below the bridge," answered the Fish. "Turn back, for your life. Do you know of a good pool within reach upward?"

"Not one," said the Stag; "but hide yourself if you can, my Lord Salmon, for the hounds will be down presently."

But for all the Salmon's warnings he went on yet a little further, for he knew that he should find another stream flowing into that wherein he stood, before he reached the bridge. So down he went till he reached it, and then without leaving the water he turned up this second stream for another mile. Then at last he went up into the covert, turning and twisting as he had seen old Aunt Yeld on the moor, and picking out every bit of stony ground, just as his mother had taught him.

Meanwhile he heard the hounds trying down the

other stream far beyond the spot where he had left it; and when at last they tried back up the water after him the evening was closing in, and the scent was so weak and all of them so tired that they could only hunt very slowly.   So he, like a cunning fellow, kept passing backward and forward through the wood from one stream to the other, till at last he began to grow tired himself; when luckily he met the Salmon again, who led him down to a deep pool, where he sunk himself under the bank, as he had once seen Aunt Yeld sink herself.   He lay there till night came and the valley was quiet and safe, and then he jumped out and lay down, very thankful to the friendly waters that had saved his life.

CHAPTER IX

Our Deer was so much pleased with himself after his escape that he began to look upon himself as quite grown up, and hastened back to the moor as soon as October came to find himself a wife. I needn't tell you that it was his old play-fellow, Ruddy's daughter, who had been born in the same year as himself, that he was thinking of; and he soon found that she wished for nothing better. But most unluckily the old Stag, whose squire he had been, had also fallen in love with her, and was determined to take her for himself. He would run after her all day, belling proposals at the top of his voice ; and his lungs were so much more powerful than our Deer's that, do what he would, our friend could not get a word in edgeways. At last the Hind was so much bored by the noise and the worry that she made up her mind to steal away with our Deer quietly one night, and run off with him under cover of the darkness ; which was what he had long been pressing her to do whenever he could find a chance.

So off they started together for the quiet valley to which the Wild-Duck had shown him the way when he was still a yearling with his mother; for there he knew that they would be undisturbed and alone, which is a thing that newly-married couples particularly enjoy. And I may tell you that if ever you hear of a stag and hind that have strayed far away from their fellows to distant coverts, you may be quite sure that they are just such another young couple as this of our story.

Of course he took her everywhere and showed her everything in the valley, explaining to her exactly how he had baffled the hounds there a few weeks before. And he tried hard to find the Salmon who had helped him so kindly, but he could not light upon him anywhere, nor find any one who knew where he was gone. The Wild-Ducks were gone to other feeding-grounds, and the only people whom he could think of who might have known were a pair of Herons that roosted in the valley; but they were so dreadfully shy that he never could get within speaking distance of them. Once he watched one of them standing on the river-bank as still as a post for a whole hour

together, till all of a sudden his long beak shot down
into the water, picked up a little wriggling trout, and
stowed it away in two seconds. Then our Stag (for
so we must call him now) making sure that he would
be affable after meals, as people generally are, trotted
down at once to talk to him. But the Heron was
so much startled that he actually dropped the trout
from his beak, mumbled out that he was in a dreadful
hurry, and flew away.

But, after they had lived in the valley a month or
more, there came a bitter hard frost, and to their joy
the Wild-Ducks came back to the river saying that
their favourite feeding-ground was frozen up. The
best chance of finding the Salmon, they said, was to
follow the water upward as far as they could go. So
up the two Deer went till the stream became so small
that they could not imagine how so big a fish could
keep afloat in it, but at last catching sight of what
seemed to be two long black bars in the water they
went closer to see what these might be. And there
sure enough was the Salmon with another Fish beside
him, but he was as different from his former self as a
stag in October is from a stag in August. The
bright silver coat was gone and had given place to a
suit of dirty rusty red; his sides, so deep and full in

the summer, were narrow and shrunken; and indeed the biggest part of him was his head, which ended in a great curved beak, not light and fine as they had seen it before, but heavy and clumsy and coarse. He seemed to be in low spirits and half ashamed of himself, but he was as courteous as ever. "Allow me to present you to my wife," he said, "though I am afraid that she is hardly fit to entertain visitors just at present."

Then the other Fish made a gentle, graceful movement with her tail, but she looked very ill and weak, and though she had no great beak like her mate she seemed, like him, to be all head and no body.

"But, my Lord Salmon," said the Stag, "what has driven you so far up the water?"

"Well, you see," said the Salmon in a low voice, "that my wife is very particular about her nursery; nothing but the finest gravel will suit her to lay her eggs on. So we came up and up, and I am bound to say that we have found a charming gravel-bed, and that the eggs are doing as well as possible; but unfortunately the water has fallen low with this frost, and we cannot get down again till the rain comes. Only yesterday a man came by and tried to spear me and my wife with a pitchfork, but luckily he slipped on the frozen ground and fell into the water himself, so that we escaped. But she was very much frightened, and till the frost breaks we shall still be in danger. Do not stay here, for it is not safe; and besides I am ashamed to see visitors when we are in such a state."

"But what about the eggs, my Lord Salmon?" said the Stag.

"The stream will take care of them; and if a few are lost, what is that among ten thousand?" said the Salmon proudly. "But let me beg you not to wait."

So the Deer went down the valley again, hoping that the West wind might soon come and drive away the frost, for the Salmon's sake as well as for their own. And a few days later they were surprised to meet the old Cock-Pheasant from Bremridge Wood, who came running towards them, very gorgeous in his very best winter plumage, but rather nervous and flurried.

"Why, Sir Phasianus," said the Stag, "what brings you so far from home?"

"Well, the fact is," said the Pheasant, "that I did not quite like the look of things this morning.

Some men came round early while I was feeding in my favourite stubble, and began beating the hedges to drive me and all my companions back into my wood. Most of those foolish Chinese birds flew back as the men wanted them, but I have not lived all these years for nothing, so I flew up the valley and have been running on ever since. Hark! I thought that I was right."

And as he spoke two faint reports came echoing up the valley; "pop! pop!" and then a pause and again "pop! pop!" a sound which was strange to the Deer.

"That's the men with their guns," said the cunning old Bird, "they are beating my wood, and that's why I am here. To-morrow they will be there again, but the next day I shall return, and I hope to have the pleasure of receiving you there very shortly after." And he ran up into the covert and hid himself under a bramble bush on a heap of dead leaves, so that you could hardly tell his neck from the live leaves or his body from the dead.

The Deer would not have thought of accepting his invitation, for they were very comfortable where they were, but that a few evenings later the air grew warmer and the South-West wind began to scream

through the bare branches over their heads. Then
the rain came down and the wind blew harder and
harder in furious gusts, till far away from them at
the head of the covert they just heard the sound of
a crash; and not long after a score of terrified
bullocks came plunging into the covert. For a beech-
tree on the covert fence had come down, smashing
the linhay in which the bullocks were lying, and
tearing a great gap in the fence itself; which had
not only scared them out of their senses but
had driven them to seek shelter in the wood. And
the Deer got up at once and moved away; for they
do not like bullocks for companions, and guessed that,
when the day came, there would be men and dogs
wandering all over the covert to drive the bullocks
back.

So they went down the valley and into Bremridge
Wood. The old Cock-Pheasant was fast asleep high
up on a larch-tree when they came, but when the day
broke he came fluttering down in spite of the rain, and
begged them to make themselves at home. For the
pompous old Bird was so full of his own importance
that he still considered himself to be master of the
whole wood and the Deer to be merely his guests.
Of course they humoured him, though their ancestors

had been lords of Bremridge Wood long before his; so the Stag complimented him on the beauty of his back, and the Hind told him that she had never seen so lovely a neck as his in her life. But still he seemed to want more compliments, though they could not think what more to say, until one day he turned the subject to dew-claws; and then he asked the Hind why her dew-claws were so much sharper than the Stag's and why they pointed straight downward, while the Stag's pointed outwards, right and left. Now these were personal questions that he had no business to put, and indeed would not have put if he had been *quite* a gentleman. But before the Hind could answer (for she had to think how she should snub him without hurting his feelings *too* much) he went on:

"And by the way, talking of dew-claws I don't think I have ever showed you my spurs." And round he turned to display them. "You will agree with me, I think," he continued, "that they are a particularly fine pair, in fact I may say the finest that you are ever likely to see."

And certainly they were very big for a pheasant, more than half an inch long, curved upward and sharp as a thorn. "I find them very useful," he added, "to keep my subjects of this wood in order. When the Chinese Cocks first invaded my kingdom they were inclined to be rebellious against my authority, but now I am happy to say that they know better." And he strutted about looking very important indeed.

Now about a week after this there was a full moon, and there came flying into the wood a number of Woodcocks. The Deer thought nothing of it, for they had often seen as many, and were always delighted to watch the little brown birds digging in the soft ground and washing their beaks in the water. But on the second morning after their arrival a Jay came flying over their heads, screeching at the top of his voice that there were strangers in the covert, and presently the old Cock-Pheasant came running up in a terrible fluster, not at all like the king of a wood.

"It's too bad," he said, "too bad. They have been here twice already, and they have no business to come again." And as he spoke there came the sound which they had once heard before, the pop! pop! of a double-barrelled gun, but this time much nearer to them, and much more alarming. The Stag jumped to his feet at once and called to the hind to come away.

"But you can't get away," said the old Pheasant, half angry, but almost ready to cry. "I have already tried to run out in half a dozen places, but wherever I went I met an odious imp of a Boy tapping two sticks together; and really a Boy tapping two sticks together is more than I can face. How I hate little Boys! But I won't stand it. I'll run back through the middle of them, and then I declare that I'll never enter this wood again. It's really past all bearing."

And he turned and ran back, but soon came forward again. "It's no use," he said, "I shall run up over the hill and take my chance. But I vow that I'll never enter this wood again. It's high time that they should know that I won't stand it."

So off he ran again, but the Deer waited and listened; and they could hear behind them a steady tapping of sticks along the whole hill-side, which came slowly closer and closer to them. And every creature in the wood came stealing forward round them, Rabbits and Cock-Pheasants and Hens and Blackbirds and Thrushes, and a score of other Birds, dodging this way and that, backward and forward, and listening with all their ears. The Deer went

forward a little way, but presently a Cock-Pheasant
came sailing high in the air over their heads. They
watched him flying on, vigorous and strong, till all
of a sudden his head dropped down, and his wings
closed; and as he fell with a crash to the ground
they heard the report of a gun ring out sharp and
angry before them. Then they hesitated to go
further, but other shots kept popping by ones and
twos behind them, till at last they turned up the
hill as the Cock-Pheasant had turned, and began to
climb steadily through the oak-coppice.

As they drew near the top of the hill they heard
more tapping just above them, and going on a little
further found the old Cock-Pheasant crouching down
just below a broad green path. And on the path
above him stood a little rosy-cheeked Boy in a ragged
cap, with a coat far too big for him and a great
comforter which hung down to his toes, beating two
sticks together and grinning with delight. The
Deer thought the Pheasant a great coward not to
run boldly past so small a creature, but, as they
waited, there came two more figures along the path
and stood close to the Boy; and the Stag remembered
them both, for they were the fair man and the
pretty girl whom he had seen when he was a calf.

The man looked a little older, for there was now a little fair hair, which was most carefully tended, on his upper lip, and he held himself very erect, with his shoulders well back and his chest thrown out. There he stood, tall and motionless, with his gun on his shoulder, watching for every movement and listening for every rustle, so still and silent that the Deer almost wondered whether he were alive. The girl stood behind him, as silent as he; and the Stag noticed as a curious thing, which he had never observed in them before, that both wore a scarf of green and black round their necks. But her face too had changed, for it was no longer that of a girl but of a beautiful woman, though just now it was sad and troubled. Her eyes never left the figure of the man before her except when now and again they filled with tears ; and then she hastily brushed the tears away with something white that she held in her hand, and looked at him again.

But all the time the tapping behind them came closer and closer, and the shots rang louder and louder, till at last the Deer could stand it no longer, and dashed across the path and up over the hill. As they passed they heard the man utter a loud halloo, and in an instant the old Cock-Pheasant was

on the wing and flying over the trees to cross the
valley. He rose higher and higher in the air, and
presently from the valley below came the report of
two shots, then again of two shots, and once more
of two shots ; and they heard the fair man laugh
loud after each shot. But the old Bird took not the
slightest notice, but flew on in the sight of the
Deer till he reached the top of the opposite hill,
where he lighted on the ground, and ran away as
fast as his legs could carry him.

Then the Deer too crossed the valley further
down, and stood in the covert watching. And they
saw a line of men in white smocks beat through the
covert to the very end, while the fair man and the
girl waited for them in the field outside. But presently another man came riding up on a pony, and
then all the men with guns came closing round the
fair man and seemed unwilling to let him go. But
after a short time he jumped on to the pony and
trotted back along the path waving his hand to them,
while they waved their hands to him. Presently he
stopped to look back and wave his hand once more,
and the girl waved her white handkerchief to him,
and then he set the pony into a gallop and disappeared. But the other men went on, and the

girl turned back by herself very slowly and sadly. Then the shots began to ring out again in the valley, and the Deer went away over the hill to the wood whence the bullocks had driven them, and finding all quiet made their home therein once more.

CHAPTER X

THEY had not been there many days when the old Cock-Pheasant came up to them and invited them back to Bremridge Wood.

"I can assure you," he said very pompously, "that you shall not be disturbed again for at least a year."

"Why, Sir Phasianus," said the Stag, "I thought you had vowed never to enter it again."

"In a moment of haste I believe that I may have done so," said the old bird; "but I have thought it over, and I cannot conceive how my wood can get on without me. How should all those foolish, timid birds look after themselves without me, their king, to direct them? No! there I was hatched, and there I must stay till I end my days. And I shall feel proud if you will join me, and stay with me, and honour my wood with your presence on—ahem!—an interesting occasion."

" Indeed ? " said the Stag.

" Yes," said the old Pheasant ; " I had the misfortune to lose my wife when the wood was shot
some weeks ago. She had not the courage to come
here with me,"—(this, I am sorry to say, was not
quite true, for he had run away alone to take care of
himself without thinking of going to fetch her)—
" and I am contemplating a new alliance—not directly, you understand—but in a couple of months
I hope to have the pleasure of presenting you to my
bride."

The Stag was much tempted to ask how he
could marry a Chinese ; and the Hind hesitated for
a moment, for, as you will find out some day, every
mother is deeply interested in a wedding. But she
and the Stag did not like to be disturbed, and they
could not trust the Cock-Pheasant's assurance after
all that had happened ; besides, she had arrangements
of her own to make for the spring. So they con-
gratulated him and bade him good-bye ; nor did
they ever see him again. And if you ask me what
became of him, I think that he must have died in
a good old age, unless, indeed, he was that very big
bird with the very long spurs that was shot by
Uncle Archie last year. For he was such a bird

as we never see nowadays, and, as he said himself, the last of his race.

So the winter wore away peacefully in the valley, and the spring came again. The Stag shed his horns earlier than in the previous year, and began to grow a finer pair than any that he had yet worn. And a little later the Hind brought him a little Calf, so that there were now three of them in the valley, and a very happy family they were. So there they stayed till quite late in the summer, and indeed they might never have moved, if they had not met the Salmon again one day when they went down to the river. He was swimming upward slowly and gracefully, his silver coat brighter than ever, and his whole form broader and deeper and handsomer in every way. He jumped clean out of the water when he saw them, and the Stag welcomed him back and asked him where he had been.

"Been?" said the Salmon, "why, down to the sea. We went down with the first flood after you left us, and merry it was in the glorious salt water. We met fish from half a dozen other rivers ; and the little fellows that you saw in their silver jackets asked to be remembered to you, though you would hardly know them now, for they are grown into big Salmon. But we were obliged to part at last and go back to our rivers, and hard work it was climbing some of the weirs down below, I can tell you; indeed, my wife could not get over one of them, and I was obliged to leave her behind. Ah, there's no place like the sea! Is there, my little fellow?" he said, looking kindly at the little Calf.

But the Hind was obliged to confess, with some shame, that her Calf had never seen the sea.

"What! an Exmoor Deer, and never seen the sea?" exclaimed the Salmon; and though he said no more, both Stag and Hind bethought them that it was high time for their Calf to see not only the sea, but the moor. So they bade the Salmon good-bye, and soon after moved out of the valley to the forest, and over the forest to the heather. And the Stag could not resist the temptation of going to look for old Bunny, so away they went to her bury. But when he got there, though he saw other Rabbits, he could perceive no sign of her; nor was it till he had asked a great many questions that one of the Rabbits said:

"Oh! you'm speaking of great-grandmother, my lord. She's in to bury, but she's got terrible old and tejious." And she popped into a hole, from which

after a while old Bunny came out. Her coat was
rusty, her teeth were very brown, and her eyes dim
with age; and at first she hardly seemed to recognise
the Stag; but she had not quite lost her tongue, for
after a time she put her head on one side and began.

"Good-day, my lord; surely it was you that my
Lady Tawny brought to see me years agone, when
you was but a little tacker. 'Tis few that comes to
see old Bunny now. Ah! she was a sweet lady, my
Lady Tawny, but her's gone. And Lady Ruddy was
nighly so sweet, but her's gone. And the old Greyhen to Badgworthy, she was a good neighbour, but
her's gone; and her poults be gone, leastways they
don't never bring no poults to see me. And my last
mate, he was caught in a net. I said to mun, 'Nets
isn't nothing;' I says, 'When you find nets over a
bury, bite a hole in mun and run through mun, as
I've a-done many times.' But he was the half of a
fule, as they all be; and he's gone. And there's my
childer and childer's childer, many of them's gone,
and those that be here won't hearken to my telling.
And—"

But here the other Rabbit cut in. "Let her
ladyship spake to 'ee, grandmother. Please not to
mind her, my lady, for she's mortal tejious."

But old Bunny went on. " Is it my Lady Tawny or my Lady Ruddy? I'm sure I can't tell. I'm old, my lady, and they won't let me spake. But I wish you good luck with your little son. Ah! the beautiful calves that I've seen, and the beautiful poults, and my own beautiful childer. But there's hounds, and there's hawks, and there's weasels and there's foxes; and there's few lasts so long as the old Bunny, and 'tis 'most time for her to go." Then she crept back slowly into the hole, and they saw her no more.

So they went on and found other deer; but Ruddy was gone, as old Bunny had said, and Aunt Yeld alone remained of the Stag's old friends. She too was now very old and grey, and her slots were worn down, and her teeth and tushes blunted with age. But the Hind and Calf were delighted to meet with deer again, and they soon made friends and were happy. But as the autumn passed away and winter began to draw on, the Stag grew anxious to return to the valley again, and would have had the Hind come too; but she begged so hard to be allowed to stay on the moor, that he could not say her no. She always lay together with other Hinds, and they gossiped so much about their calves that the Stag took to the company of other stags on Dunkery; but

he always had a craving to get back to the valley for
the winter, and after a few weeks he went back there
by himself.

And lucky it was for him, as it chanced, for in
January there came a great storm of snow, which for
three weeks covered the moor, blotting out every
fence and every little hollow in an unbroken, trackless
waste of white.   The deer on the forest were hard put
to it for food, and even our Stag in the valley was
obliged to go far afield.   But he soon found out the
hay-mows where the fodder was cut for the bullocks,
and helped himself freely ; nor was he ashamed now
and then to take some of the turnips that had been
laid out for the sheep, when he could find them.   So
he passed well through the hard weather, and when
the snow melted and the streams came pouring down
in heavy flood, he saw the old Salmon come sailing
down in his dirty red suit, and thought that, though
both of them had been through hard times, he had
got through them the better of the two.

Then the spring came and he began to grow sleek
and fat ; and, when he shed his horns, the new ones
began once more to grow far larger than ever before.
So he settled down for a luxurious summer, and took
the best of everything in the fields all round the

coverts. And when the late summer came he found that he needed a big tree to help him to rub the velvet from his horns, so he chose a fine young oak and went round it so often, rubbing and fraying and polishing, that he fairly cut the bark off from all round the trunk and left the tree to die.

One morning, soon after he had cleaned his head, he went out to feed in the fields as usual, and had just made his lair in the covert for the day, when he was aware of a man, who came along one of the paths with his eyes on the ground. The Stag waited till he was gone, and then quietly rose and left the valley for the open moor. For he had a shrewd suspicion that all was not right when a man came round looking for his slot in the early morning; and he was wise, for a few hours later the men and hounds came and searched for him everywhere. And he heard them from his resting-place trying the valley high and low, and chuckled to himself when he thought how foolish the man was who thought to harbour him in such a fashion.

But after this he left the valley for good, and went back to the coverts that overhung the sea, where he hid himself so cunningly day after day that he was never found during the whole of that season.

And when October came and the deer began to herd together, he looked about for his wife, but he could not find her anywhere, and he had sad misgivings that the hounds might have driven her away, or worse, while he was away in the valley. His only comfort was the reflection that if he wished to marry again, and he and another stag should fancy the same bride, he could fight for her instead of stealing her away. All that winter he lay on Dunkery with other stags, as big as himself and bigger, for he was now a fine Deer, and began to take his place with the lords of the herd. And he grew cunning too, for he soon found out that hinds and not stags are hunted in the winter-time, and he did not distress himself by running hard when there was no occasion for it. He would hear the hounds chasing in the woods quite close to him and never move.

One winter's day when he was lying in a patch of gorse with three others, he heard the hounds come running so directly towards him that in spite of himself he raised his head to listen. And immediately after, old Aunt Yeld came up in the greatest distress, and lay down close to them. An old stag next to her was just rising to drive her off, when a hound spoke so close to them that they all dropped their chins to the ground and lay like stones. And poor Aunt Yeld whispered piteously, "Oh! get up and run; I am so tired; do help me." But not a stag would move, and our Stag, I am sorry to say, lay as still as the rest. Then the hounds came within five yards of them, but still they lay fast, till poor Aunt Yeld jumped up in despair and ran off. "May you never know the day," she said, "when you shall ask for help and find none! But the brown peat-stream, I know, will be my friend." And she flung down the hill to the water in desperation, with the hounds hard after her; and they never saw her again.

So the Stag lived on in the woods above the cliffs and on the forest for two years longer. Each year found his head heavier and bearing more points, his back broader, his body heavier and sleeker, and his slots greater and rounder and blunter. He knew of all the best feeding-grounds, so he was always well nourished, and he had learned of so many secure hiding-places in the cliff from the old stag whom he had served as squire, that he was rarely disturbed. More than once he was roused by the hounds in spite of all that he could do, but he would turn out every deer in the covert sooner than run himself; and when, notwithstanding all his tricks, he

was one day forced into the open, he ran cunningly
up and down the water as his mother had showed
him, and so got a good start of the hounds. Then
he cantered on till he caught the wind of a lot of
hinds and calves and dashed straight into the middle
of them, frightening them out of their lives. He
never remembered how much he had disliked to be
disturbed in this way when he was a calf; he only
thought that the hounds would scatter in all directions after the herd. And so they did, while he
cantered on to the old home where he had known
the Vixen and the Badger, took a good bath, and then
lay down chuckling at his own cleverness.

A very selfish old fellow you will call him, and I
think you are right; but unluckily stags do become
selfish as they grow older. But he always kept to
the chivalrous rule that the post of honour in a retreat
is the rear-guard, and always ran behind the hinds
when roused with a herd of them by the hounds.
Still, selfish he was, and though he had profited by all
of Aunt Yeld's early lessons, he forgot until too late
the last words that she had spoken to him, even
though as a calf he had once saved her life.

CHAPTER XI

ONE beautiful morning at the very end of September our Stag was lying in the short plantations above the cliffs in a warm sunny bed of which he had long been very fond, when his ear was disturbed, as had so often happened before, by the cry of hounds. He did not mind it so much now, for he knew that it meant at any rate that they were hunting some other deer than himself. And it was plain to him that they had found the stag that they wanted, for not two or three couple but seventeen or eighteen were speaking to the scent. Therefore he lay quite still, never doubting that before long they would leave the covert. And so it seemed that it would be, for presently the cry ceased, and he had good reason to hope that they had gone away. The only thing that disquieted him was that the horses seemed always to be moving all over the plantation, instead of galloping over the moor. He was still

lying fast when he heard two horses come trotting
up to within thirty yards of his lair; and peering
carefully through the branches he saw them and
recognised them. One of them was the fair man
whom he had seen so often before, still riding the
same grey horse, which was grown so light as to be
almost white. But the man was greatly changed.
His face was thin and hollow, and would have been
pale if it had not been burnt brown; the tiny hair
on the upper lip had grown to a great red moustache;
and the blue eyes were sunk deep in his head.
And he rode with his reins in his right hand, for his
left was hung in a sling, so that he could hardly hold
his whip. But for all that he was as quick and
lively as ever, and his eyes never ceased roving over
the plantation. And by him rode the beautiful girl
whom he had seen with him before, her face aglow
with happiness; and she seemed so proud of him that
she never took her eyes off his face for an instant,
except now and then to glance pityingly at his
wounded hand. They pulled up not far from the
Stag and waited.

And presently a hind came up, cantering
anxiously through the plantation, for she had laid her
calf down and did not wish to go far from him.

She blundered on so close to the Stag that he would have got up and driven her away if he had not been afraid of being seen. But she passed on, and very soon the hounds came up after her. Then the man brought the white horse across them, trying hard to stop them from her line, but he could not use his whip ; and they only swerved past him, still running hard, straight to the bed of the Stag. And up he jumped, his glossy coat gleaming bright in the sun, and every hound leaped forward with a cry of exultation as he rose.

He went off at the top of his speed straight through the plantation, for he knew that he had the better of the hounds through the thicket. But they ran harder than he had ever known since the day when they had driven him to sea as a yearling, and, as he could wind no other deer, he made up his mind to cross the moor for the friendly valley where he had lived so long. So turning his head from the sea he leaped out of the plantation, and ran down to the water below. He would gladly have taken a bath then and there, but the hounds were too close ; so splashing boldly through it he cantered aslant up the steep hill beyond as though it had been level ground. And when he gained the top, he felt the West wind strike cool upon him, and saw the long waves of heather and grass rise before him till they met the sky. Then he set his face bravely for the highest point, for beyond it was the refuge that he sought.

And on he went, and on and on, cantering steadily but very fast, for though he heard no sound of their tongues he knew that the hounds were racing after him, as mute as mice. The blackcock fled away screaming before him, the hawk high in air wheeled aside as he passed, but on he went through the sweet, pink heather, without pausing to notice them. Then the heather became sparse and thin, growing only in ragged tufts amid the rank red grass and sheets of white bog-flower. He had lain in this wet ground many times, but no deer was there to help him to-day. Then the wet ground was passed and the heather came again, sound and firm, sloping down to a brown peat-stream. Never had its song sounded so sweet in his ears, never had he longed more for a bath in the amber water, but the hounds were still racing and he dared not wait. So he splashed on through the stream and up another ridge, where the heather grew but thinly amid a wilderness of hot stones. The sun smote fiercely

upon him, and the air was close as he cantered down
from the ridge into the combe beyond it, but he
cared not, for he knew that there again was water.
He ran up it for a few yards, but only for a few
yards, for the hounds were still running their hardest,
and he must wait till the great slope of grass before
him was past.

So he breasted it gallantly, up, and up, and up.
The grass was thick over the treacherous ground,
but his foot was still too light to pierce it, and he
cantered steadily on. His mouth was growing parched,
but he still felt strong, and he knew that when the
hill was crossed he would find more water to welcome
him. At last he reached the summit, and there
spread out before him were Dartmoor and the sea,
and far, far below him the haven of his choice; and
the cool breeze from the sea breathed upon his nostrils,
and he gathered strength and hope. There was still
one more hollow to be crossed before he reached the
long slope down to the valley, but there was water
in it, and he might have time for a hasty draught.
So still he pressed on with the same steady stride,
hoping that he might wait at any rate for a few
minutes in the stream, for thirst and heat were growing upon him, and he longed for a bath. But no!

it was dangerous to wait ; and he turned away sick
at heart from the sparkling ripple, and faced the
ascent before him. And now the grass seemed to
coil wickedly round his dew-claws as if striving to
hold them down ; and he tugged his feet impatiently
from its grasp, though more than once he had half
a mind to turn back to the water. But he had
chosen his refuge, and he struggled gamely on.

At last he was at the top, and only one long
unbroken slope of heather lay between him and the
valley that he knew so well; and he turned into a
long, deep combe which ran down to it, that he
might not be seen. Down, and down, and down he
ran, steadying himself and recovering his breath. At
every stride he saw the trickle of water from the head
of the combe grow larger and larger as other trickles
joined it from every side, and he knew that he was
near his refuge at last. Presently he came upon a
patch of yellow gorse, which had thrust up its
flaming head through the heather, and he plunged
heavily through it, knowing that it would check
the hounds. Another few hundred yards and he
was within the covert, in the cool deep shade of the
oak-coppice, with the merry river brawling beneath
him

And he scrambled down eagerly through the trees and plunged into the brown water. How delicious it was after that fierce race over the heather, running cool and full and strong under the shadow of the coppice! He hardly paused to drink, but ran straight down stream, for his heart misgave him that the hounds had gained on him while he was struggling up the last steep ascent. And the water carried him on, now racing down his dew-claws, now lapping round his hocks, now rising quiet and still almost to his mane, sometimes for a few seconds raising him off his weary legs and bearing him gently down.

Only too soon he heard the deep voice of the hounds throwing their tongues as they entered the wood, but he kept running steadily down, refreshed at every step by the sweet, cool water, and screened from all view by the canopy of hazel and alder that overhung it. At last he left it, and turning up into the woods ran on through them down the valley. Once he tried to scale the hill to the next valley, but he found the air hot and stifling under the dense green leaves, and he felt so much distressed that he turned back and continued his way down. Presently there rose up faintly behind him the deep note that he knew so well of the old black and tan hound; then the voices

of other hounds chimed in together with it, and he
knew that they had hit the place at which he had
left the water. He heard the sound of the horn
come floating down the valley, and tried hard to
mend his pace, but he could not; and at last he was
fain to leave the wood and come back to the water.

Again he ran down, and again the friendly stream
coursed round him and revived him. So he splashed
on for a time and then he sought the woods anew in
hope of finding help, but he could not stay in them
long, and returned once more to the water. At last,
on turning round a bend in the stream, he came upon
a Heron, standing watching for eels, and he cried out
to him, " Oh ! stand still. I won't hurt you. Stand
still till the hounds come, and the men will think
that I have not passed." But the Heron was too shy
to listen, and flapped heavily away. Then he came
to a bridge, where his passage was barred by a pole,
but he threw his horns back and managed to jump
between the pole and the arch, without touching
anything, and though he could not help splashing the
pole, he made his way down without leaving the
water.

At length he came to the end of the woods, and
here he hesitated, longing for some one to tell him

about the stream further down, for it was strange to him. And he remembered Aunt Yeld's words, " May you never know what it is to look for help and to find none." But he could hear nothing of the hounds, and almost began to hope that he might have beaten them. So at last he found a corner thickly overhung with branches, and there he lay down in the water. And then whom should he see but the Lady Salmon making her way slowly up the stream, the very friend who could tell him what he wanted to know.

But before he could speak to her she said, " Beware of going further down, for there is a flood-gate across the stream which you cannot pass. Have you seen my husband ? "

And he told her, " Yes," and she swam on, while he lay still and made up his mind where he would go if the hounds came on. The hounds indeed had dropped behind him, for the men could not believe that the Deer could have leaped the pole under the bridge, and had taken them to try for him somewhere else. But the old black and tan hound had tried to walk along the pole to wind it before they came up, and having fallen into the water and been swept on past the bridge, was still trying downward by himself.

And thus it was that while the Deer was lying in the water the old hound came up alone. He seemed to have made up his mind that the Stag was near, for he stopped and kept sniffing round him in all directions till at last he crept in under the bank, caught sight of him, and threw his head into the air with a loud triumphant bay. The Stag leaped to his feet in an instant and dashed at him, but the old hound shrank back and saved himself; and then the Stag broke out of the water, for he had made up his mind to breast the hill, and push on for Bremridge Wood. He knew the way, for it was that which the Partridge had shown him, and he felt that by a great effort he could reach it.

And as he slanted painfully up the steep ascent he heard the old hound still baying with disappointment and rage; for he could not scramble up the steep bank so quickly as the Deer, and the more he bayed the further he was left behind. Further up the valley the Stag could hear the horn and hallooing of men, but he pressed on bravely and gained the top of the hill at last. But when he reached it his neck was bowed, his tongue was parched, and his legs staggered under him. Still he struggled on. He was in the enclosed country now, but he knew every field and every rack, and he scrambled over the banks and hurled himself over the gates as pluckily as if he had but just been roused. Thus at last he reached the familiar wood. A Jay flew screaming before him as he entered it, but he heeded her not. His head was beginning to swim, but he still knew the densest quarter of the covert and made his way to it. The brambles clutched at him and the branches tripped him at every step, yet he never paused, but shook them off and went crashing and blundering on, till at length with one gigantic leap he hurled himself into the thickest of the underwood and lay fast.

After a time he heard the note of a hound entering the wood, and he knew the voice, but he lay still. Then other hounds came up speaking also, and he heard them working slowly towards his hiding-place. But as they drew near the thicket the voices were less numerous, and only a few hounds seemed to have strength and courage to face it. He caught the voice of the black and tan hound speaking fitfully as he came nearer and nearer, and more impatiently as he struggled with the brambles and binders that barred his way. At last it reached the place from which he had leaped into his refuge, and there it fell silent. Still the hound cast on, and from a path far above came the voice of a man encouraging him, and encouraging other hounds to help him. But the Deer lay like a stone, while the hounds tried all round within only a few yards of him, when all of a sudden the old hound caught the wind of him and made a bound at him where he lay. The Deer jumped to his feet and faced him, and the old hound bayed again with triumph, but dared not come within reach. So there they stood for two whole minutes till the other hounds came up all round him. Then one hound in his insolence came too near, and in an instant the Deer reared up, and plunging his antlers deep into his side, fairly pinned him to the ground, so that the hound never moved again. Then he broke through the rest of them, spurning them wide with horn and hoof, and crashed on through the covert towards the valley.

And as he came to the edge of the wood he heard the song of the peat-stream rise before him, and knew that he had still one refuge left. Reeling and desperate he scrambled out of the wood and leaped down into the park at its foot. The Fallow-Deer were not to be seen, for they had heard the cry of the hounds in the wood and had hidden themselves in alarm among the trees, but the Stag heard the voice of the stream calling to him louder than he had ever heard it, and he heeded nought else. And he ran towards the place where he heard it call loudest, and found it rushing round a bend, very smoothly and quietly, but very swiftly. At every foot below it seemed to rush faster, till fifty yards down it struck against a bridge of three arches, through which it raced like a cataract and poured down with a thundering roar into a boiling pool beneath.

And the Stag leaped in and set his back against some alders that grew on the opposite bank, choosing his place cunningly where he could stand but the hounds must swim. Then he clenched his teeth and threw back his head, and dared his enemies to do their worst. And the brown stream washed merrily round him, singing low, but as sweetly as he had ever heard it.

" *Come down with me, come. Oh ! merry and free*
Is the race from the forest away to the sea.
The pool is before me ; I hark to its call
And I hasten my speed for the leap o'er the fall.
The Salmon are waiting impatient below,
I feel them spring upward as over I go.
Come down with me, come ; why linger you here ?
You know me, the friend of the wild Red-Deer."

Then the voice of the water was broken, for the black and tan hound came bounding down in advance of the rest over the grass to the water, caught view of the Deer where he stood, and throwing up his head bayed loud and deep and long. And other hounds came hurrying down through the wood, speaking quick and short, for they were mad with impatience; and bursting through the fence straight to the black and tan hound they joined their voices in exultation to his. Then a few, a very few, men came up hastening with what speed they might on their weary, hobbling horses, a man on a white horse leading them, and they added their wild yells to the baying of the hounds, while ever and anon the shrill tones of the horn rose high above them all in short, quick, jubilant notes. Soon some of the hounds grew tired of baying in front and flew round to the bank behind him, still yelling fiercely in impotent rage; and the maddening clamour rang far up the valley through the sweet, still evening. The Fallow-Deer huddled themselves close among the trees, and the pigeons hushed their cooing and flew swift and high in the air from the terror of the sound. But the Stag stood unmoved in the midst of the baying ring, with his noble head thrown back and his chin raised scornfully aloft, in all the pride and majesty of defiance.

But all the while the stream kept pressing him downward inch by inch, very gently but very surely. Once a hound, in his impatience, burst through the branches and ran out on the stem of an alder almost on to his back, so that he was obliged to move down still lower. And there the stream pressed him still more strongly, though never unkindly, and he went downward faster than before ; and he heard the full voice of the torrent, as it thundered over the fall, chanting to him grand and sonorous in a deep tone of command.

> " *Nay, tarry no longer, come down, come down*
> *To the pool that invites you, still, peaceful, and brown.*
> *One plunge through the rush of the shivering spray*
> *And the dark, solemn eddies shall bear you away*
> *From the rustle of bubbles, the hissing of foam,*
> *To a haven of rest, and a long, long home.*
> *Come down with me, come ; your refuge is near ;*
> *I call you, the friend of the wild Red-Deer.*"

And he heard it and yielded. The water rose higher, and the strength of the current grew more urgent about him, till at length the stream lifted him gently off his weary feet and bore him silently down. For a moment he strove with all his might to stem the smooth, impetuous tide as it swept him on ; then he gave himself up to the friendly waters, and throwing his head high in air in a last defiance, he went down swiftly over the fall.

And the wild baying ceased ; and he heard nothing but the chorus of the waters in his ears. Once he struggled to raise his head, and the great brown antlers came looming up for a moment through the eddies ; but as he passed down to the deep, still pool beyond the fall, the water called to him so kindly that he could not but obey.

" *From my wild forest-cradle, through deep and through shoal,*
You have followed me far, and have reached to the goal.
Now the gallop is ended, the chase it is run,
The struggle is over, the victory won.
The fall is o'er-leaped and the rapids are passed,
Come rest on my bosom untroubled at last.
Nay, raise not your head, come, bury it here ;
No friend like the stream to the wild Red-Deer."

So the waters closed over the stern, sharp antlers, and he bowed his head and was at peace.

Then men came and pulled the great still body out of the water ; and they took his head and hung it up in memory of so great a run and so gallant a Stag

But their triumph was only over the empty shell of him, for his spirit had gone to the still brown pool. And indeed the stream has received many another wild deer besides him, which, I suspect, is the reason why ferns, that love the water, take the shape of stags' horns and of harts' tongues. So there he remains ; for he had fought his fight and run his course ; and he asks for nothing better than to hear the river sing to him all the day long.

The Hill of the Red Fox

Allan Campbell McLean

'Unknown man found shot' said the newspaper headline. Alasdair recognised the man he had met on the train to Skye, the man who had slipped him a desperate last message 'Hunt at the Hill of the Red Fox M15'.

Alasdair finds the Hill of the Red Fox on Skye, but the note still makes no sense. Nor at first do most of the strange and dangerous goings on on the island, many of which involve Alasdair's sinister uncle, Murdo Beaton. There is much more than the odd bit of poaching happening—atomic scientists and their secrets are disappearing.

People are not always what they seem. Whom can Alasdair really trust? In finding out he uncovers a web of espionage—and all its perils!

ISBN 0 86241 055 X   (age 10+)   £1.95

Escape from Loch Leven

Mollie Hunter

When Mary, Queen of Scots, arrives at Loch Leven Castle, a reluctant 'guest' at the mercy of her treacherous lords, it is not long before her legendary beauty and charm win the hearts of her captors and the passionate devotion of young Will Douglas, the orphan page boy.

Yet for all the elaborate schemes of her loyal band of followers, it is the ingenuity and courage of the young page which secure her release and the chance to regain her crown.

There can be few who do not know the final fate of the tragic young queen, yet Mollie Hunter has succeeded in recapturing the atmosphere of intrigue, excitement and hope which surrounded her in captivity.

ISBN 0 86241 137 8   (age 11+)   £1.95

Haki the Shetland Pony

Kathleen Fidler

There is no future for Adam Cromarty on his parents' croft in the Shetlands. Should he sell his beloved pony Haki, whom he has cared for and trained since birth, to buy a ticket for the mainland where there is more chance of a job? Adam cannot bring himself to do this so he makes a deal with a circus owner that he can only buy Haki if he takes him too as trainer.

They settle well into the different but exciting life of the circus and Haki is a great success with the audience. But Adam makes a bitter enemy: Willy Baxter, in charge of the chimps, is jealous of Adam's success. He tries to injure Haki and eventually succeeds, although the circus elephant, with whom Haki has an extraordinary relationship, steps in to prevent total disaster.

"This is a gripping and sometimes heart-rending tale. The plot and characterisation of both people and animals are first rate— Kathleen Fidler has excelled herself again."

ISBN 0 86241 075 4 (age 8 +)   £1.75